A Minute for Me

Learning to Savor Sixty Seconds

A Minute for Me

Learning to Savor Sixty Seconds

Megan McDonough

SATYA HOUSE PUBLICATIONS

Hardwick, Massachusetts

Previously published work

Infinity in a Box: Using Yoga to Live with EASE

This publication is available at special discounts for bulk purchases for educational needs. Customizing options are available upon request. For details, write:

Satya House Publications
P. O. Box 122
Hardwick, Massachusetts 01037
orders@satyahouse.com § www.satyahouse.com

Publisher's Cataloging-In-Publication Data
(Prepared by The Donohue Group, Inc.)

McDonough, Megan.
    A minute for me : learning to savor sixty seconds / Megan McDonough.

    p. ; cm.

    Available also as a shorter POD version and an ebook. Additional content available in this print version.
    ISBN: 978-1-935874-09-6

    1. Conduct of life. 2. Self-realization. 3. Self-help techniques. 4. Quality of life. I. Title.

BF637.C5 M23 2012
158.1

Acknowledgements

Life is so much richer and more rewarding when you have supportive friends and family. I'm blessed to have such wonderful people in my life.

When I write, my mind is focused on what's being created in front of me. Everything else is a distraction. My husband and two children have put up with my lack of attention when my eyes are glued to the computer monitor. I love you dearly. I appreciate your good humor and understanding when the writing takes center stage. And I love that many of the stories I write start right here at home. Thanks for all the great inspiration.

Writing is not the only task to create this book you hold in your hands. After I'm done (I think) with the writing, someone else takes a gander to see what ghastly mistakes I've made. Tresca Weinstein, editor with the eagle eyes, is the gentle soul whose skills always improve my writing. Tresca and I worked together on many writing projects for the Kripalu Yoga Teachers Association. I am so thrilled she could also work with me on this book.

To take the writing out of the virtual computer space and move it into material existence, a midwife—sometimes known as a publisher—is needed. I am, as always, grateful to Julie Murkette, publisher and dear friend. You make life so much easier.

To everyone who read the early version and gave me valuable feedback—Joan Peters, Dedie King, Soleil Hepner, Vandita Kate Marchesiello, Nischala Joy Devi, Elissa Cobb and Karen Hasskarl. I admire you all so much, and continue to be inspired by the work you bring so compassionately and completely into the world. Thanks for being such powerful role models and for taking time to give back so generously.

These days, after a book finally comes out in paper form, it's time to turn right around and put it back into the virtual space so it can spread across the globe (at least that's every author's hope). My good friends at YogaHub.com have made it easy for me to create a virtual community. Many thanks go to Segovia Smith and Christina Souza Ma for building such an inclusive and complete virtual home. As super as that site is, it doesn't hold a candle to how super it is to have friends like you. Our work together continues to be a creative blast.

Finally, to the wonderful yoga students who bless me with their presence in class and in life. I love sharing that sacred space with you.

And thank you for reading these words. Without you, the writing would be incomplete. All writing needs a reader. May you enjoy the experience of reading as much as I enjoyed the writing.

Table of Contents

How to Take *"A Minute for Me"*

"Shaken, not stirred," was the way James Bond took his martini break in those not-too-frequent moments of rest between steamy sex and spy action. How do you take your own brand of rest and rejuvenation? How do you take a minute for yourself in a hectic day?

We are a driven society, consumed with action and rewarding those who get things done. The more you can get done—for your family, at your job, in your community—the more you are seen as productive. You're seen as pulling your weight.

The high price for getting things done can be letting your self become undone.

Does it have to be that way? Do you need to work like a dog, trading your own health and well-being to gain financial security? Do promotions mean sacrificing your family life? Does doing your duty mean you desert yourself? Does living a responsible life demand the ransom of never-ending must-do's?

I sincerely hope not. I'm betting that the more you are able to balance your own needs with the demands of others, the more you will be able to give—and to receive in return.

What is "A Minute for Me"?

Taking "A Minute for Me" means we find space—some distance from the demands, a stillness or quiet spot—just to reconnect with ourself. Even if we are feeling absolutely hemmed in by circumstance, or overwhelmed with responsibility, we can begin by looking at where space already exists. We can start our day with the inquiry, "Where is the space in this day, in this moment, for me?"

Can we still feel, sense, and stay connected to self in all the busyness?

Maybe there's "A Minute for Me" when you first wake up in the morning or just before you fall asleep at night. Maybe that minute comes when you are taking a shower or going for a walk. Maybe that minute comes just by the simple act of taking a deep breath. Or maybe your minute comes when you change your mind about something that has troubled you.

If you watch closely, somewhere, sometime, somehow, there are moments just for you. If we are mentally busy, though, these quiet spaces can quickly be drowned out by the thoughts of what else you need to do for your children, for work, or for your spouse.

The more you actively pay attention to finding "A Minute for Me" the more moments you'll have.

It's important to cultivate that self-awareness even in busy times, when it feels like nothing else can be crammed into the day. Because at some point in your life, you will most surely be alone. Just you and empty blocks of time hanging out like old pals. Maybe it will be when the kids leave for college. Or you divorce a spouse of many years. Or, as will come to all of us at one time or another, when we face death alone.

That long-awaited quiet time comes—and we'll have no idea what to do with it. Who are you without this list of to-do's?

After a lifetime ignoring or suppressing our own self and needs, there's only a void where our vibrant self should be.

This book is about staying connected to the most important person in your life—you. And we're going to do that by bringing yourself back to you even as you attend to all of life's demands.

Rather than a time-out, try a time-in.

For years people have been telling me I should read the *New York Times* best-seller *Eat, Pray, Love* by Elizabeth Gilbert. I finally cracked the book open after one of my senior yoga students gave it to me, with yet another endorsement of "you'll love this."

She's right, it's a great book.

The author writes about doing what many long for—finding a connection to self and to the divine. She finds that connection in a year-long travel of self-discovery in far-away lands.

I'll admit to feeling fleeting pangs of jealously when I first started reading. Who wouldn't want to travel to exotic places, meet esoteric gurus and medicine men, all while trying to figure out who they are?

The pangs of jealously lifted when I realized what I would refuse to trade for such an adventure. I love taking care of my family, being there for my children when they get off the bus from school, and making dinner (well, maybe that's a stretch, but you get the picture). I love my work teaching, writing, and consulting. I love my little country town where I know everyone's name.

The exotic path others take to self-exploration is not my path. Mine is much more . . . average. Or maybe the more accurate word is mundane.

The mundane, average, everyday circumstances can be a doorway to the big questions like who you are and where you're going in this lifetime. Life is, just as it is, our biggest teacher. Your life is your path. That's the thing to honor, the thing that deserves your attention.

For self-discovery, exotic travel is optional. Inquiry is mandatory.

That's why this book is not about giving answers—how presumptuous would that be? Instead, it's filled with questions, inviting you to inquire about what is true for you. Along with personal stories to motivate your own exploration and inquiry, you'll find simple 60-second exercises to build that "minute for me" muscle into your day. Building that muscle is absolutely critical to living an authentic life. Self-discovery is the only path back to you.

Many times it's impossible to "escape," to get away physically from the demands of life. But you can plan a mental escape. You can mentally change your focus from the outside—the *gazillion* things you think you need to do—and hone your focus on the one thing that you are doing in this very moment. Take a "time-in" this moment.

You can think about the past, you can plan for the future, but the only time you experience life is right now. This is as good as it gets! Life is always happening now. If you are constantly re-running the "to-do" list through your mind, or rushing to get one thing done so you can do something else, you miss this moment. In the blink of an eye, life goes by and you wonder how you got to be that person in the mirror.

If James Bond can take time to sip a fancy martini between sex scenes and death threats, there's a "minute for me" somewhere in your day. Or, if the philosophy of Thoreau speaks more to you than Hollywood's 007, there is time to "live deliberately."

Maybe that is the ultimate exotic travel—the exploration of your own heart.

Directions

Since when does a book need directions? It's fairly straight-forward—open the cover, read each page, and move from beginning to end.

You could read this book in that traditional way, I suppose. But what I really want—what I really hope to accomplish with this book—is for you to be deeply engaged in your own experience. That only comes about when you shift your perspective from what you are reading to the inner experience of *how it relates to you.*

That means shifting your attention from the words on this page to what's happening inside you this very moment. You are the center of attention here, not the book.

So directions are needed because you are not reading the way you have always read. Instead of reading words, you are reading your heart. You are exploring *you,* and this book is just a way of prompting you to bring your attention to many different facets of self.

Here's how the journey unfolds. . . .

Each mini-chapter has two components: a story and a reflection. The story can be read in under a minute and is meant to be a fun and light-hearted way of approaching the things that happen every day. These stories come from my life, with the hope that you can find some similarities that relate to your life. The reflection time comes after the story, and it's called *A Minute for Me*.

The reflection is the turning point from standard reading to self-inquiry. What does this reading mean to me? How does it play out in my life?

When you come to A Minute for Me reflection, do yourself a favor and take a deep breath in, let it out with a sigh, and feel your body relax. Turn your attention inward, and mentally shift gears from reading to observing what's happening inside.

Then read the reflection and ponder the questions.

There's space below each reflection area to journal or to doodle. You can also feel free to ignore the blank area and instead stare off into space or sit quietly.

What's not written is so much more important than what is written. What's not written is your story. That's the only story that ever matters. And you've got to take the time to decipher it for yourself. No one else can author that writing but you.

You can read each story and reflection sequentially, or you can open the book up at some random point and start there. There is no beginning or end. There's just constant self-inquiry. You are a very interesting story, with lots to explore.

A Minute for Me

Keep Quiet Now. Pay Later.

My daughter broke her arm after falling off a horse. Not a minor break, mind you, but a bend-your-elbow-backwards type that required surgery. She broke both bones in her lower arm, dislocated her elbow, and broke off a bone fragment that had to be screwed back in place.

It's not an experience either of us ever wants to go through again.

While we were in the emergency room, Emily's arm needed to be set so that the elbow would pop back into place. As my husband and I tried to comfort her, the team worked on setting her up for the procedure.

An IV was started for the pain medication. Right away Emily started complaining about the pain from the IV. I thought it odd that she would complain about such a minor thing compared to how much the other arm must hurt. A thought floated through my mind: "Is the IV set properly?"

I know a bit about IV's since I used to put them in when I worked at a hospital. But as I looked around that crowded room I saw an orthopedic physician, an orthopedic resident, an ER doctor, an ER resident, and an ER nurse. Surely they knew what they were doing.

So I kept my mouth shut.

The pain medication was started, dripping slowly into the IV. When the doctor touched Emily's arm to set it, she screamed in pain. Obviously the medication wasn't working. They increased the medication and got the same result. So they increased it again. Still Emily screamed. And as tears rolled down my cheeks as I witnessed my daughter's pain, I continued to dismiss the thought "The IV is set wrong."

The dosage of pain medication was almost to the max. The next dose would be Emily's last. Finally the ER doctor said, "Let me just check the IV."

I'll bet you know what comes next.

The IV was infiltrated, meaning the pain medication was not getting into the vein where it could do its job.

On top of the sorrow I was feeling for my daughter's suffering, I now had a heaping load of guilt for not speaking up in the face of authority. By remaining silent, I had added to my daughter's pain.

How often do we silence that inner voice, thinking that others surely know more than we do? How often do we assume that it's our perspective that's faulty?

That night in the ER, I got a big, sickening dose of what happens when I dismiss my inner questions instead of giving them voice. I could have just asked to check the IV. Instead I remained silent.

Why don't we speak our truth? For fear of hurting someone else? Because we don't want to create an uncomfortable situation? Because we're afraid to expose ourselves?

Are we creating pain—for ourselves or for others—with our silence?

My daughter's arm is fine now. She's healthy, happy, and pain-free. After the crisis was over, we had a chat about the moments leading up to the accident, when she made the decision to run the horse through open fields instead of simply walking down the street. I asked her what that little voice in her heart had said just before she entered the field.

"Mommy," Emily said, "that little voice told me it was not such a good idea." She was with an older friend, however, and kept that opinion to herself.

I know exactly how she felt.

A Minute for Me: Speaking Your Truth

Notice today when you hedge your bet, skirt around an issue, or beat around the bush in order to avoid a potentially awkward situation.

When do you muffle your own truth? Do you keep quiet because you see another's opinion as more valid or deserving? Or perhaps fear or uncertainty holds you back? Or perhaps you don't speak because you think the other person knows the truth (as I thought with the doctors in the emergency room).

How do you encourage or discourage others from expressing their truth? Are you open to hearing it? Even if it seems awkward and trivial, practice slipping in little tidbits of your personal truth. That truth may be as simple as telling the waiter that the meal was disappointing, rather than giving the usual pat reply of "fine".

How would expressing your truth, without exaggerating or dramatizing, change your experience?

A Minute for Me

From Manure to Armani

To the veterinarian coming to check out our horse Rocky's lame hoof, I looked like your typical farmhand. Sporting a very stylish and flattering one-piece Carhart snowsuit, fat felt-pack L.L. Bean boots, a gray wool hat pulled low over my ears, and hands tucked into matching wool gloves, I was the big brown female version of the Michelin tire guy. Watch out *Baywatch*, guys, I'm way hot—temperature-wise, that is.

But underneath the not-so-seductive brown suit, I wore a white cashmere sweater, black dress pants and, tucked into my boots, nylons instead of wool socks. After Dr. Mark was done, I played Clark Kent. I whipped off the hat and mittens, zipped out of the canvas coveralls, and threw on a black-and-white suit coat. I tossed the felt-packs down cellar and slipped on leather loafers. Then, like Superman, I flew off to my business meeting.

I wonder if my colleagues could smell horse manure.

Just like Clark Kent, I felt the power that comes from almost magically changing identity, in this case from farmer to corporate executive.

How many roles do you play in life? Is there room for all that you are, all the identities that allow you to express the many facets of who you are?

Everybody has different talents and interests that like to come out and play. Sometimes I crave being outside in nature—taking care of the horses and dogs and making maple syrup on the farm. Other times sitting in front of a fire with a book is heaven. On some days, teaching yoga is just what I need; on others, business meetings can feel creative and constructive. Through it all, playing the role of mother and homemaker brings a sense of continuity.

But if I play any one role for too long without a break, I get cranky. What was satisfying becomes a chore. Too much mothering can be draining; too much work makes Jack a dull boy; too much of any one thing becomes bland. Just as with food, rotation and moderation lead to balance.

Feelings of being trapped, a sense of monotony, or a "same shift, different day" attitude are all sure signs that other interests are being stifled.

You may not move from manure shoveler to corporate trainer, but does your day have a changing rhythm? What roles do you move between in the course of the day? What is your relationship to each of these roles?

Like Superman's spandex and my Michelin Man getup, the uniforms that go with your roles may vary widely—or not at all. The question is how comfortably each one fits, and whether your transitions from one to the next are as effortless as slipping in and out of a phone booth.

A Minute for Me: Changing Roles

Notice the places of transition today, when you shed one role for another. Take sixty seconds and notice the transition when you walk through the door after work, transitioning from worker to parent or partner. Or a minute when you transition from being a customer to serving the customer.

What different states of mind are needed for each role? How does giving yourself a minute to observe the transition prepare you for that new role?

Book Burning

After my first book was published, I had an idea as I lay in bed one morning: I was going to burn that sucker in a big old fire. I was going to turn that hard work into ash.

I usually use the time between sleep and waking to let my mind wander where it will, without limits or controls. That particular morning my mind decided to play with the soon-to-be-released book. I imagined holding the words I had strung together over the course of years in the form of a finished book. I considered how vulnerable I would feel reading it to others during a promotional tour. And I pondered the most devious question of all: Will it sell?

It's a devious question because there are other questions hidden in what looks like a purely financial concern. The implied question: Is the book worthwhile? Is it meaningful? And hidden even deeper, the darkest question of all: Am I worthwhile? Am I valued? Am I meaningful?

That's when the idea flashed into my mind: burn it. I even began plotting out the scene of the crime. I'd wait until my husband and children left the house, lest they think Mommy had lost her marbles. I'd light a big bonfire that wouldn't leave a trace, and toss that book right on in.

We all have our pet projects. Things we've invested a lot of ourselves in. Whether it's building our dream house or working for many years at your job, these projects become representations of who we are, embodying our hopes, dreams, desires, and fears. The mistake for me came when I mistook my book as a representation of who I am.

The book will stand on its own (or not). Yes, I'll support it as I can as it moves out into the world, but my relationship with it has changed. It's no longer my little baby to hold close. It's no longer about me, if it ever was.

Perhaps this cycle happens in all relationships. When our children grow and leave home, when a spouse heads in a different direction than we would have chosen, or when a long career ends in retirement, it leaves us with the need to redefine ourselves. If we don't, then we're struggling to hold on to what is no longer ours.

What are you holding onto that needs to stand on its own? Write it out on as many pages as you need, staple it together, and go have a bonfire.

A Minute for Me: Wake Up!

There is a transitional moment that exists first thing in the morning when you wake up. Before the mind clicks on and we start thinking about the day's schedule, there is a quiet time where the mind is awake from sleep, but not yet dialed into the rush of the day.

Take a minute to notice that spot.

Explore what happens when the mind moves from sleep to wakefulness to high speed. How long does that transition take? What is the body's response to these mind-states? What is the impact of noticing the moment? Does your observation change the moment?

My Rhythm. Our Rhythm.

The thought crossed my mind, in singer Todd Rundgren's words, "I don't want to work, I just want to bang on the drums all day."

So I did.

Drummers Shaun Laframboise and Allison Gemmel of Hands Down Drumming ran a program for those of us who wanted to welcome in the New Year by banging on a drum. Although I had never played the drums before—besides the proverbial pots and pans kids are always banging on—I came out of the program actually able to keep a rhythm going.

Not bad for a rhythm-challenged, two-left-thumbs pot-smacker.

At one point in the program, our group of newbies was asked to join the seasoned professionals as they drummed for an audience of dancers. The room was a beehive of buzzing motion. Wild dancers rocked the hall. The air vibrated with the soul-splitting thumping of an African drumbeat pounded out by more than forty drummers.

I had to close my eyes. The sound was wonderfully overwhelming.

Learning the new beat, I had to keep two conflicting ideas in my mind. First, I had to completely block out the other drummers and stay focused on my rhythm. I had to listen only to my part if I wanted to play it correctly, and not get confused by someone else's beat. At the same time, I had to be aware of the overall beat of the group. All the parts had to come together into one, so that my individual role integrated into the cohesive whole.

This, of course, is a metaphor for life. How do you stay true to your own unique beat while engaging in the music of a group, a community, a family, a country, a planet?

Your family, friends, coworkers, and neighbors all play a melody. Are you aware of that melody? Do you feel a part of the song, able to maintain your own rhythm while contributing to the rhythm of the whole? Do you pull back from the group because you feel it threatens your personal rhythm?

Initially it takes a great deal of focused attention to hear and honor your own beat, and even more to meld it with the group melody. But as you become more attuned to your own beat, and that of the group, it becomes easier to stay in your own truth and playfully interact with the group rhythm.

Think of it this way. When you plant a new lawn, the grass is vulnerable. The young green sprouts can be damaged simply by being walked on. Care for your lawn, though, and with time, space, and water, you'll eventually be able to have a horse graze on it without hurting the grass.

Care enough for your own beat to let it grow. Then enjoy the fun and ecstasy of jamming with others who are playing their beats for all to hear, joining together to create a single glorious heartbeat.

A Minute for Me: Listening To Your Beat

Becoming attuned to your own beat takes attention to detail—especially the detail of emotion.

Sound is the result of playing an instrument. Emotions can be the result of a given direction or thought process. When you do something aligned with the rhythm of life, it feels good. Emotions like happiness and satisfaction naturally arise. Fall out of alignment, and fight the rhythm, and you'll feel lousy.

What do your emotions tell you about your alignment (or not) with the rhythm of life?

Today, watch your emotions as indicators of alignment. When you act, think, or speak in alignment with your own beat (which could also be called your own truth) what emotions are present? What happens to your emotions when your thoughts, actions or words are misaligned?

Waiting For Maple

This has been a tough season for the New England maple syrup industry. First the weather was unseasonably cold, too cold for the sap to run. Then the weather turned too warm too fast, further delaying the sap. I know this because my husband Joe and I run a small sugarhouse where we make the world's best maple syrup (she said ever so humbly).

Joe has been frustrated with Mother Nature this season. There isn't much he can do, however. The weather will be what it will be, so right now we're in a waiting mode. While he's keeping a close eye on the weather reports and staying close to home in case the sap runs, Joe is finding that his days are different than he'd expected. This time of year he's usually boiling sap at odd hours rather than sitting around waiting.

There are times in life when we have little or no control over circumstances, and all we can do is wait. Wait for the results of a job interview, wait to hear from a family member after we've written a letter of reconciliation, wait for the impending reorganization at work to see if we still have a job, wait for our child to come home after she took the car out for the first time.

Waiting can create anxiety. Not being able to take action to influence an outcome can lead to excess energy that has no outlet. I think that's why my husband has been pacing through the house, at a loss as to what to do next while waiting for the sap to flow.

Is there a way to use waiting time effectively?

There are benefits to waiting. For instance, this maple season has allowed our family to spend more time together. Waiting time can be used for reflection, slowing down into the present. Many times, by relaxing into the waiting, we can see that anxiety stems from our worried projections into the future. Anticipating what might happen next usually manufactures stress.

How we view today comes from yesterday's thoughts, and our present thoughts of today build our view of tomorrow: Life, then, is a creation of our mind. The next time your anxiety level rises when you're standing in line, sitting in a traffic jam, or waiting out a life situation, see if you can find a hidden benefit. Sink into the present moment of waiting by keeping your thoughts focused on now.

A Minute for Me: Waiting

What does waiting feel like? When you notice a sense of waiting today, finish the sentences below.

I am waiting for . . .

I'm waiting for something (or someone else) because in this moment I'm *(bored, anxious, worried, excited, unhappy with what I'm currently doing, lonely, etc.).*

The sense of waiting gives me . . .

Without the sense of waiting, I would . . .

Wasting Time with a Guru

Last week I went to see a guru, a man who was billed as an expert on Internet marketing. I cleared my schedule and spent the whole afternoon in a large conference room with a crowd of other eager learners. Sitting in the front row so I could hear every word he said, I waited for the wisdom to flow. The first fifteen minutes surprised me. By the end of the second fifteen minutes, I was restless. An hour in, I was yawning. When was he going to stop talking about his superstar accomplishments and start teaching?

Not too long after that, I had a conversation with a yoga student. She told me that she had found liberation by simply saying "no" to expert advice that didn't fit her style.

It would be nice if the answers to our problems could be handed to us on a silver platter by a wise guru. But that's pure fantasy. The only place where your truth resides is in you.

The best guidance any guru can offer, whether he or she is a business expert or a spiritual leader, is to point you in the direction of your own self. Gurus can do that by being a shining example or a hideous caricature. In either case, they are simply pointing back at you, reflecting what you aspire to be or what you rebel against.

Yup, it's all about you. Beyond the judgments about "good" gurus and "bad" gurus, something else quietly lives. In yoga class, we touch this place when we lie in relaxation. In life, we know this place when we acknowledge the truth of our own experience.

If the purpose of a guru is to show us our own self, then each person we come across is a guru. In that case, there are no "good" gurus and "bad" gurus. There are only mirrors in which we see our own faces.

A Minute for Me: Listening 100%

We tend to give our full attention to those we deem as powerful—whether we call them gurus, experts, politicians or celebrities. We listen at the edge of our seat when they speak.

What would happen if we gave everyday people this amount of focused attention by listening to what they had to say?

During your next conversation, practice the art of concentrated listening. So often we try to get our opinion in, offer our perspective, tell our story or give advice, that we miss the opportunity to be completely immersed in listening 100%.

Imagine how relaxing it could be to simply listen, without the responsibility of solving a problem or reciprocating with equal talking time.

For deep listening, practice being a mirror. Reflect back what you hear, giving yourself the opportunity to really appreciate what is being said while you give the other person the gift of their own wisdom. To encourage your active listening, say things like:

"Tell me more about that. . . ."
"What I hear you saying is . . . ."
"I hear you."
"How did that sit with you?"
"What else?"

You can also just repeat a few keys words or phrases that have been spoken (without being really obnoxious or obvious!).

Notice your own reaction when you listen without needing to contribute. What arises when you can just bear witness in a conversation without needing to control it?

Going with the Flow

This week my husband and I took down the maple syrup tubing on our farm. These tubes connect the maple trees so that when the sap is flowing, it travels through the tubing system into collection tanks. Gone are the days of the quaint metal buckets collecting sap drop by drop.

Before taking down the tubing, we need to wash it. As we pull out the spouts that connect the tubing to each tree, water is forced through the system by a pump. The pressure is strongest near the source, making the water scream out of the first spout. Further down the pipeline there's no pressure at all, and no water flows out. When I began the process, I ran around the woods like a mad person, quickly trying to reach all the different spouts.

In life, pressure can keep us running back and forth just as frenetically. It seems like we get one area under control and a dam breaks someplace else. We even have clichés that point to the progressive nature of bad luck: "Everything happens at once," and "Bad things come in threes."

By the time Joe and I made it to the last sugar bush, I understood the system of pressure in the tubing. By starting at the main line, I could easily work with the water, moving with its natural flow rather than running from one spot to another in a haphazard way.

The flow of life, like the flow of water through tubing, has its own natural rhythm. In order to understand your own rhythm, you simply need to observe it. Right now, reading this, is your energy distracted by other tasks that vie for your attention? Is your energy fully engaged in reading? Is the flow of your energy right now constructive or destructive?

Looking at your life as a conscious flow of energy gives you the option of blocking off the spouts that drain you. You also have the choice to open and say yes to what energizes and enlivens you.

Another well-worn cliché strikes at the truth: "Go with the flow."

There is a beginning, middle and end to everything. Each breath, thought, emotion, life, day, and night has a beginning, a middle and an end.

A Minute for Me: Art Fun

Let's have some fun with art today. This little exercise helps focus the mind while going with the flow.

Pick out something in front of you that has interesting detail and bring it close enough to you so you can really see it.

Take a blank piece of paper and a pen or pencil. Put the pen to paper and leave it there for the duration of the exercise. For the next sixty seconds, let your eyes follow the object in front of you while your pen follows the eye movement by drawing on the paper. Keep your eyes on the object and the pen on the paper. You'll be tempted to glance at the paper to see what you're drawing. Don't do it.

When the minute is up, take a look at what you drew. What was it like focusing your mind so much on one thing while allowing the hand to draw? What details were you able to discern? What is the relationship between the image and the real thing? Could your hand relax in the process since you went with the flow and didn't care about the outcome? How does this process apply in life?

Confessions of a Potato Chip Junkie

Here's a confession: I'm a potato chip junkie. I love the salty taste and crisp crunch of chips. I can eat a whole bag if left to my own devices, hearing my mind the whole time thinking, "You should stop now." I indulge, and then my body feels uncomfortable, stuffed, and unhealthy. You'd think I'd know better by now, but just last night I had pizza and way too many chips.

Hours later, I was suffering. My body worked overtime trying to digest the fat and complained loudly the whole time, warning me not to do it again. I vowed never to eat another chip, and to throw away the bag I still had in the cabinet.

This morning I felt back to my healthy self, with the vow still fresh in my mind. I didn't even crave a chip. Later, though, when I was packing for a family picnic at a nearby park, I saw the chips. I thought about throwing them away, but that seemed like heresy—very wasteful indeed. I noticed that my mind was not as revolted by the idea of eating a chip as it had been last night, when I was in pain. For a brief moment, I even considered eating a few.

That thought is laughable.

My body's not addicted to chips; my thinking is addicted to chips. When the pain of chip abuse was fresh, my thoughts strongly rejected eating more. Once the pain receded, my thoughts became friends with the chips again. This tells me one thing: my thoughts cannot be trusted.

The chip abuse needs thought intervention.

Do you have a pattern of thoughts that oscillate back and forth, causing you grief? Whether it's a yo-yo diet, an internal struggle about staying with or leaving your mate, or the debate about finding a new job versus staying in your current job, the problem comes up when we believe that our thoughts are telling us the truth.

What if we accepted the idea that thoughts are as fickle as the wind, changing with the circumstances? When I feel good, my thoughts say, "Have some chips." When I feel bad, my thoughts say, "Never eat chips again." It can drive a person crazy. Heap on top of that the negative thoughts that arise when a chip is finally eaten, and you start to realize it's not the chips that are the problem: it's those slippery thoughts about the chips.

What if, instead of focusing on our obsession, we focus on the thoughts about the obsession? Would understanding the nature of our thoughts change our relationship to our obsession?

I'm off now to throw away that bag of chips.

Or maybe not.

A Minute for Me: Sixty-Second Starvation

When you sit down at your next meal, take a sixty-second break. Instead of diving right into eating, take a moment to look at the food. How is it arranged on the plate? What is the color palette of the food?

Notice the smell. How does the smell affect your feelings of hunger? Does the smell heighten anticipation?

Be aware of sensations. What does hunger feel like? Where is it located in the body? What thoughts are arising about waiting to eat? How do those thoughts affect sensations?

How does the urge to eat push you? Can that push be placated, at least for a moment? Hold off eating for a full minute, and notice how that changes the meal. When you do actually place the food in your mouth, take a 60-second taste. Take time to chew, to feel the texture of the food, to really taste it, before you swallow.

A Minute for Me

Mother Teresa and Hitler

I was lucky enough to teach yoga at the first national convention of World WIT (Women, Insight, Technology). During one of the general sessions, futurist Edie Weiner spoke about trends and where they were heading. She wove together a spectrum of fascinating facts on a variety of subjects, ranging from water supply issues to politics to nanotechnology. This woman knew her stuff. At one point she posed this question to the group: "What did Hitler and Mother Teresa have in common?"

That got our attention. There was a collective intake of breath from the audience. We were sitting on the edge of our seats. The mere act of putting those two names together in the same sentence, much less the same breath, seemed like sacrilege.

How could those two people be in any way alike?

Weiner compared them from the perspective of leadership. And no one would argue that Hitler and Mother Teresa were outstanding leaders. From two different ends of the value spectrum, to be sure, but nonetheless phenomenal leaders.

Here's what they had in common.

First, both were passionate about what they believed in. Second, both had amazing communication skills for getting that passion across to others. But it was the third point that blew me away.

According to Weiner, both Mother Teresa and Hitler had a complete lack of embarrassment when it came to promoting their respective passions.

Have there been times in your life when you've hedged your words because you were embarrassed to speak your truth? When have you avoided taking a risk for fear of embarrassment? Have you ever let a marketing or sales opportunity go by because you were embarrassed about seeming too pushy? Or failed to speak up in a group because you were afraid you'd be embarrassed by your lack of knowledge?

If you're like me, there have been plenty of times that embarrassment has gotten in your way, keeping you from stepping out into the world and into your truth. Being embarrassed by who we are, what kind of car we drive, what we do or say, or how we look and act can causes us to retreat, pulling back from life.

What would happen if each time embarrassment arose you greeted it as a sign that you needed to move forward? What if, instead of retreating from the possibility of embarrassment, you rode straight though it?

What would happen in your life if you acknowledged embarrassment without indulging it, if you took strong action despite your discomfort?

Would embarrassment disappear, leaving only conviction in its place?

A Minute for Me: Fear of Embarrassment

Take a moment and remember when you were really embarrassed. How many occasions can you remember?

Now think about the times you worried about being embarrassed, so you stopped short and didn't expose that particular vulnerability.

Which occurs more often, fear of embarrassment or embarrassment itself?

Is fear of embarrassment stopping you from stepping out? What's the worst embarrassment that could happen? Could you live with that?

Superman: Ride of Steel

During spring break, I took the kids to Six Flags Amusement Park, home of Superman: Ride of Steel. I love roller coasters, but haven't been on one in eons. So when I saw the towering steel frame of one of the fastest and tallest roller coasters in the world, I knew it was time for a ride.

As the roller coaster started climbing, nothing obstructed the dizzying view from my seat straight down to the Connecticut River. I remember feeling as a child the pure adrenaline rush of excitement when riding a roller coaster. As an adult, I felt the pure adrenaline rush of fear.

I prayed as the top few cars sunk out of sight. When my car rocketed down the tracks at 80 miles an hour, my screaming voice was left behind along with my stomach.

I never felt closer to God as I repeated wildly in my head, "Please let it stay on the track, please let it stay on the track, please let it stay on the track. . . . "

That day, thank heaven, Superman stayed on track. A week later, though, a man died on that same ride after being ejected from his seat.

Life—and amusement park rides—offers no guarantees.

Have there been times when you've felt that your life is completely out of your control? No matter how frightening the ride, no matter how twisted and curvy, no matter how much you wish whoever's in control would slow down, stop, and let you off, there's no getting out.

Times of such intensity wipe away apathy. In extreme situations there's no mask to hide behind, no energy for playing useless games. The raw stuff of life that is usually well protected and hidden comes rushing to the surface, and it's here that we discover who we are.

Lift your arms, scream and shout, pray to whatever you call God. In the face of fear, the ride of life goes on. Surrender, and see what comes around the next bend.

A Minute for Me: The Un-Superman

Life feels like the opposite of the adrenaline-filled superman ride when dull and monotonous routines lull us into lethargy.

Behavior creates habits, and habits in return reinforce behavior. Before we know it, life is like a repeating record instead of a glorious adventure. There's only one way out: break the habit.

Today's minute is quite simple. Start your day differently. Whether it's skipping the morning e-mail check, taking a different way to work, or refusing to argue with your teenage son, do the opposite of your norm. Watch your habit trying to resurface, and the effort it takes to take a new course.

In what ways do your habits serve you? In what ways are they detrimental?

Let the Universe Breathe You

I felt an asthma attack coming on this morning as I was teaching yoga. It came at the worst possible moment, just as I was getting ready to lead the final relaxation. I had been neglecting to use the steroid inhaler that keeps my asthma in check. When I feel good, I forget that I need it. When I have difficulty breathing, I remember too late to take it, since it needs time to work. It's like having a leaky roof. Can't fix the roof when it's raining . . . no need to if it isn't.

Short of breath, I wondered how I would be able to lead the guided relaxation before the final meditation. Really, who can relax with an out-of-breath asthmatic rasping out instructions?

I started beating myself up for forgetting my medicine, while at the same time wondering how I could gracefully escape the room to use my emergency inhaler, which leaves me shaky and jittery.

Silence filled the room instead of my usual calm speaking voice.

Then the words came. As is usually the case when I'm leading relaxation, I wasn't sure what was going to come out of my mouth. Then this thought arose and I spoke it into the room: *What if the universe was breathing you instead of you trying to breathe?*

Instead of you inhaling, what if the universe was exhaling into your body everything you need in this very moment? Instead of you exhaling, what if the universe was inhaling out of you all the stuff that clogs you up?

Breathing in, you are filled with whatever you need. Breathing out, the universe takes whatever is not serving you.

Call it mouth-to-mouth with Mother Earth.

Try an experiment today. Imagine that every decision and every action (or every indecision or non-action) is exactly the right response. The wind blows when it blows, and is still when it is still. You make a decision or you don't. All striving falls away.

What would happen if you led your life without feeling that you needed to fix anything, go anywhere, or be anybody? What if you trusted that the universe was always right there for you, cleansing and providing? What if you were an empty vessel, breath moving through you, your essence merging with the universe?

Mind you, I'll be much more diligent about taking my medicine now. The universe has, after all, provided the inhaler as well as the relaxation that ended my asthma attack today.

How perfect is that?

A Minute for Me: Let It Be

It may be difficult to practice surrendering when your list to do is longer than you are tall.

Practice the art of surrender in this moment and you'll find it easier to do when daily demands threaten suffocation. One simple way to practice the art of surrendering is to do a body scan.

A body scan involves just taking your attention to specific parts of the body. This focuses the mind and relaxes the body.

Read these words to yourself. As you do, imagine that your mind is traveling to these places in your body. Let your mind touch that spot, just paying attention to it.

Notice the top of your head; the center of your forehead; the tip of your nose. Notice your top lip and your bottom lip. Notice your bottom jaw; the chin. Be aware of the throat. Notice both shoulders; your elbows, wrists and all ten fingers. Be aware of the torso; the beating heart; the waves of breath coming in and out of your lungs.

Be aware of the belly, the navel, the lower abdomen. Notice the pelvis and the hips. Feel the body sinking down into the chair. Let the back rest against the support of the chair. Bring awareness to both thighs, knees, shins, calves and all ten toes.

Notice your body from the top of your head to the tips of your toes. Let it all be and just notice the physical body as it sits in this chair.

Take a big breath in and sigh it away. As the breath falls out of its own accord, let the rest of your day release with the same ease as that exhale.

Can't Stop Snoring

Let me share a secret with you that, until recently, only my husband knew.

I snore.

It's not very dainty, ladylike, or in keeping with the image I'd like to create, but it's the truth. And this week my husband wasn't the only one affected by my snoring. I was attending a Yoga Teachers Conference, staying in the dormitory accommodations. All through the night, my roommates kept waking me to keep me from snoring. I tried unsuccessfully to stop, embarrassed that I was disturbing others. That embarrassment turned into frustration as exhaustion set in.

I couldn't stop snoring, whether my roommates continued to poke me or I tried to wake myself. I considered this the next day as I looked out the window at the mountains and lake. I wonder how many times I've poked and prodded someone, trying to get them to stop doing something that they didn't have the ability to stop.

As a manager in the corporate world, as a mother of two small children, and as a wife, how many times have I asked the impossible without realizing it? As others wrestled with their inability to change a behavior pattern, their frustration turned to anger against me, the person who kept prodding them to stop.

Here's a fact: if we could stop doing whatever we do that causes ourselves and others pain, we would stop. It's as simple as that. Everyone wants to be happy. No one wants to suffer, or to make loved ones suffer. When have you accused others of failing to make a change that you want them to make? When have you been unable to break a habit that you know is causing unhappiness for you and for others?

Most of us have been in both roles at different times—the accuser and the accused. Both represent a place of innocence, not guilt. We do the best we can. And we work with what we've got, like it or not.

For me, that meant moving into the "snoring dorm," where I slept soundly the next night among six wonderful women, all of us snoring happily together.

A Minute for Me: Judge and Jury

Today's reflection time is focused in what we all do best: judge. From the moment we wake up until the time we go to bed, we judge. That's not an admonishment, just an admission of fact. The mind is really good at making judgments. That's its job.

When you judge today, notice. It is as simple as that. There's no need to change the judgment, or justify why it is valid. Just notice.

What are you judging?

How does that judgment affect your response to that which is being judged?

Can the judgment be so automatic that it is hard to discern? Is it a very "quiet" judgment?

Are some judgments very "loud" in your mind, creating an instant feeling of like or dislike?

Turning a Snake into a Rope

International spiritual leader Byron Katie came to the little historic town of Northampton, Massachusetts yesterday. I was among the hundreds of people who packed into a hotel ballroom to watch her work her magic on the audience. If you've never heard her story before, here's the quick version. She was a depressed and suicidal woman. As she lay on the floor one day in a halfway house, feeling too unworthy to sleep in a bed, a cockroach scuttled over her foot. She came to an instant and life-changing realization: her thoughts were causing all her suffering. Since that point, she has been teaching people how to break free of their pain using a process called *The Work*.

I guess cockroaches do have a place in the universe.

Katie (yes, she goes by her last name) told us a parable that stuck with me. You're in the desert, walking along minding your own business. All of a sudden, you see a snake right in front of you. You jump back, having all the normal reactions—sweating, racing heart, adrenaline pumping. Upon closer inspection, though, you discover the snake is actually a rope.

The point of the story? Just try and be afraid of that rope again. It's impossible. Once you realize that the thing you fear is harmless, you can never recapture that moment of intense fear.

The snake/rope analogy is a classic yoga teaching. The sage Patanjali describes five kinds of thoughts, one of which is wrong knowledge. Even though a perception may feel very real and true, wrong knowledge is not based on the true nature of an object.

When you understand that the snake is only a rope, you've gained proper perspective. Have you ever tossed and turned and fretted over a situation only to realize that you were worrying about something that didn't exist? As a parent, I notice this when my imagination turns my child's simple cold into rheumatic fever. As an entrepreneur, I do this when I waste mental energy stressing out about meeting a deadline instead of just doing the job.

When do you turn a rope into a snake?

A Minute for Me: Weaving a Story

Notice today when your mind starts weaving a story that doesn't exist anywhere but in your imagination. It's interesting how often this happens once you begin to watch for it.

In your mind a talk with the boss turns into a well-deserved raise, or a bad evaluation. A trip on the steps turns into broken teeth as you imagine what could have happened. Your child's desire to be alone turns into depression as you think about it.

Watch as the mind takes you into pure fantasy. You can use this weaving story to make heaven or hell, and it all begins with thought. Like the drama in the soap opera *As the World Turns*, catch your mind as thought turns.

The Definition of Courage

My little town has a little library. A small octagonal stone structure, it's open on Tuesday night, half a day on Thursday, and a few hours on Saturday. You can get any book you want there, as long as you're patient enough to wait for the bookmobile delivery. It's a great place, and my children and I are frequent visitors.

This past week we went and filled up our book bag with new titles, bringing them home to our yard, where we spread out a blanket under the Indian-summer sun. The first book I pulled out was called *Courage*. Before we started reading, I asked my children what the word courage meant to them. My then eight-year-old daughter gave me the best definition I've ever heard. Courage, she said, is "something that holds you together."

Courage is an obvious virtue in a fearless explorer like Ernest Shackleton or a brave athlete like Lance Armstrong. Emily's definition, however, speaks of an everyday courage—a quiet courage known only to its owner, invisible to others.

"Something that holds you together" is different than "I'm holding it together."

When "I'm holding it together," it's a strained feeling, as if I can keep things in control through sheer will. This sensation comes up when I'm feeling impatient, but trying to be patient; when I'm feeling angry, but trying to be polite; when I'm feeling tired, but trying to be active.

Come to think of it, when "I'm holding it all together," I'm usually pretending to be something I'm not.

What if, instead of the strength of will, it's the act of willingness itself that's courageous? Being willing means trusting in something other than your own will to hold you together. And trusting in something other than yourself takes great courage.

A Minute for Me: Hold it Together

At some point today, you'll try to hold it together. Freeze time and really look at that sensation. When you "hold it together" what sensations arise in the body? What are you saying to yourself? Why is it necessary to hold it together? What would be the result of not holding it together? How does that belief affect your experience? Could there be "something else" responsible for holding it together? If so, could you trust that "something else" to do a good job? How would trusting affect your experience?

Hidden Ambivalence

Recently, I had the good fortune to attend a teleconference with marketing guru Jay Conrad Levinson, the icon behind the Guerilla Marketing book series. Get this: he only works three days a week. When someone asked him when he was going to retire, he answered, "I've been retired for years."

Is it a myth that we have to work like dogs for most of our life so we can "rest" at the end?

My father worked hard to build up his own food brokerage business. Two weeks after he sold his business in preparation for retirement, he died of a massive heart attack on the first hole of the golf course.

He's not alone. Statistics show that the greatest mortality occurs during the first years of retirement.

Is this what we're working so hard for?

I had a personal epiphany when I heard Levinson say he was already retired. In a sense, I consider myself retired as well. I gave up the norms of what a career "should" look like, and created a work life that suits my needs and interests. However, I didn't realize until that teleconference that I'm still harboring some ambivalence about that decision.

I wonder sometimes if I made the right choice in starting my own business. I wonder if I did the right thing by my family and children. I wonder if the price I pay for health insurance can possibly get any higher.

There are times in life when a path seems crystal clear. After a heart attack, many patients change their eating and exercise habits in an instant. Some people diagnosed with asthma quit smoking in a snap. A close call with death can make the value of life immediately clear. These are the times when there's no inner debate. The choice is clear and action is taken.

Sometimes, though, beneath what is seemingly clear lies a hidden ambivalence that can thwart the most decisive action. Doubting, questioning, second-guessing, and should-haves eat away at your goals. Unless you address that hidden ambivalence, you'll never get where you say you want to go, because you don't really want to go there with your whole heart.

Is hidden ambivalence undermining your actions?

When you feel ambivalence arising, don't repress it. Don't indulge it. Don't pressure yourself to reconcile it. Just consciously put it aside. You can always pick it up again later, if you really want to.

A Minute for Me:
Getting Out of Your Own Way

Be very aware today of thoughts that counteract a given direction. This takes great discernment, as the counteracting thoughts come at . . . well, they come at the speed of thought.

Here's an example. Every kitchen or office has a junk drawer. It's universal. You open the junk drawer in your desk or kitchen. A thought arises that you should clean the drawer out. Immediately after that another thought counteracts it, saying something like "I don't have time," or "I really don't feel like it," or "Why can't someone else clean this out once in a while?"

Before you know it, the urge to clean out the drawer has been squelched.

What if you didn't counteract that first thought? What if you allowed yourself sixty seconds to follow that original thought before discarding it?

We're used to muffling thoughts. What would happen if you gave yourself a little room—just sixty seconds—to follow the thought before gagging it? Would that practice extend to others whispers of intuition that went previously unheard?

This Indecision's Killing Me

The title of the presentation promised the impossible—and it was. "Five Thousand Years of Yoga in Fifty Minutes" was the name of the presentation I attended at a Yoga and Buddhism conference. The speaker gave a brilliant overview of the history of yoga, but my mind was getting full and I considered skipping the next session in favor of a whirlpool and sauna.

I vacillated between the two choices—like the song says, "Should I stay or should I go?" The conference speakers were world-class: what an opportunity to learn. On the other hand, the chance to drop the scheduled activity and indulge was calling me. Like another song says, "This indecision's killing me."

I watched my mind as I left the Main Hall. Back and forth the thoughts went, arguing against one another. One thought pattern supplied the pros and cons of staying; the next evaluated the pros and cons of leaving. As I watched the tennis match of opposing thoughts, I wondered, "What would happen if I didn't choose sides?"

My brain was buzzing, but there were also other things to notice. Like the fact that I had to go to the ladies' room. I followed that impulse. Afterwards, as I wandered down the hall, curiosity replaced the inner argument. Still not consciously choosing sides, I became curious as to what the next moment held. As I found myself slipping off my shoes and walking into the yoga studio, I realized the decision had been made: I was attending the next yoga session.

We can literally torture ourselves with the need to make a decision. In a stale relationship the arguing thoughts can sound a like a debate team. Should I stay or should I go? A new job opportunity arises and the lifestyle change it would impose paralyzes the mind. Should I stay or should I go? The mind, doing what it does best, tries to rationalize and figure out the "right" move.

But is that really how this thing called life works? How, for instance, have you ended up here, now, with this job, in this relationship, or in this life circumstance? How did it come to be that you are reading these words right now? Was it completely planned? Did you "make" all the decisions?

Some things, perhaps most things, simply unfold.

Try this experiment. The next time you're at an impasse and find yourself going back and forth on a decision, don't choose sides. Decide to be indecisive. See what happens to your mind. Watch where your feet take you.

A Minute for Me: Making a Decision

Today you'll make a million decisions—from what to wear in the morning to what to eat for lunch to what time to go to bed to everything in between.

Is there a logical flow of decisions from a rational mind, or are decisions based on the domino affect—one action creates the next? Does that decision making process change depending on what is being decided? Do you consciously play more of a role in one decision-making process that another? Why is it okay to let some decisions make themselves while others we feel the need to hem and haw over? What is the difference between those two decisions that makes the inner feeling so different?

Naked

As I was picking up my mail this week, I ran into one of my yoga students. Used to seeing me in yoga pants and a big T-shirt, she hardly recognized me in my business suit. She laughed, commenting on how different I looked.

Of course, people who know me only in my business suit might be hard-pressed to visualize me upside down in my yoga digs holding the Downward Dog posture. I laughed with my student and quipped, "Underneath it all I'm just naked."

That was more than she needed to know, she replied.

We all play different roles during the course of the day, moving from leader to follower, from creative thinker to organizer and taskmaster, from parent to lover. Each role comes with a different "uniform," a different way of presenting yourself in that particular scenario.

But when it comes right down to it, we are all naked beneath our costumes of life.

Sometimes we wear one costume so long it's hard to see ourselves as anything other than the role we play. Take the 30-year veteran who gets canned right before retirement. Or the high-powered executive who just gave birth to a baby girl and trades her DKNY suits for a sweat suit that is stained with spit-up by 8 A.M. Or the executive who struggles to fit his creative, artistic side into his all-consuming corporate life. Or the woman who leaves the comfort of a cushy job to start her own business.

Each of these roles demands more than a change of clothes. They demand a change in thinking. But beneath it all is the essential "you." One yoga master describes the essential self as "Not that. Not that. Not that." The roles you play are not you.

By a process of elimination, you begin to expose the subtle, quiet, powerful stillness that is you. A you that is unchanged, regardless of what uniform you wear.

You are not a business suit, or a yoga outfit, or a stained sweat suit. You are even more than just your birthday suit.

A Minute for Me: Costume Change

As you get dressed this morning, what role are you suiting up for?

There's a difference when you suit up for work versus exercise. How does each suit affect the next action you take? Are you hesitant to go for a walk in your business suit, thinking it inappropriate for exercise? Do you not go out to the post office in sweats, thinking it too messy to be seen?

Bottom line: notice today how the costume affects the roles you accept and the roles you reject. Could changing your role be as simple as changing your costume?

Vacuuming with Pearls

Did June Cleaver really wear pearls when she was vacuuming? Yes, according to the television portrayal of the perfect mother in the 1960s show *Leave it to Beaver*. Along with that string of pearls over a meticulous dress, June's neat bob was perfectly coiffed. I'm sure her domestic perfection was a curse to the "real" women of her day.

Women—and men—still struggle today under cultural norms, ideas of how parenting, relationships, and life should look. It's draining, keeping up with an illusion.

The other day, we went on a family car trip. The two kids were in the back seat arguing as ferociously as only siblings can, with my husband and me taking turns getting angry at the children and then at each other. We were the antithesis of the Cleavers.

Rather than keeping up the façade of what a family trip should be like, I decided to just name the truth of our experience. I said, "We have one impatient Mom, one angry Father, and two fighting children in this car." The kids stopped their bickering for a moment and I said, "We have two quiet children in the car." What started as a desperate attempt on my part to maintain sanity ended up being a game, with the kids joining in, naming their experience as we drove along.

As we played the game, it was evident how often our emotions changed. During the course of one short trip, we moved through anger, laughter, quiet, talking, debating, fighting, and a few other states of being. Yoga philosophy says that everything changes, constantly. I lived that, and realized it, during that car trip.

Illusions of what a holiday should look like, how clean our house should be, the clothes our children should wear, the schools they should attend, the raise we should get at work, how we think our boss should treat us, all cause strife. Stress arises when our thoughts fight what is. My thoughts claimed, "Our family trip should be peaceful." The reality was far from it.

What causes more pain, thinking that our lives should look a certain way, or experiencing the truth of our lives?

A Minute for Me: Name That State

For your minute today, practice naming the states that are arising in you. It's interesting to see how close we can come with a word that describes a certain experience. The experience of love feels different than the experience of like which is different than bliss. At some point in our collective ancestry, someone decided that "love" meant this experience, the word "like" means this experience and so on. We even created a thing called a dictionary to make sure we're all in agreement of what concept those combination of letters denote.

Words, or concepts, are meant to tease out the way we experience this moment. First comes the experience, and then comes the naming of the experience.

As you read these words, what word captures your experience?

Being Body

This week I went to a panel discussion sponsored by the holistic center where I teach yoga. The topic was "Being in Your Body" and the panelists were an odd assortment of people—ranging from stonemasons to yoga teachers, dancers, and musicians. Each had a unique story to tell about what it means to "be in your body."

One panelist told the story of how she became a paraplegic. In her struggle with intense, unrelenting pain, her perception of body changed. The question, she said, isn't "How can we be in our body"? The question is, "Can we 'be body'"?

When I heard that, a light bulb went on in my head. It made perfect sense. The idea of "being in your body" means something is split. Some part of you is invested in being "I" so that this "I" can be in the body. What if the "I" was erased and all that was left was "being body"? Or being mind? Or being thoughts? Or being breath?

At some point, many of us tackle the big existential questions: What is the purpose of my life? Why am I here? Or, even bigger still, "Am I?"—which questions our whole self.

As these words are written, I'm aware of the tapping of my fingers on the keyboard. I feel each keypad as my pointer fingers hop from spot to spot, jabbing the letters. The laptop resting on my thighs is heavy and warm.

I could lose myself in this simple act. When I do that, the existential questions fade and dissolve, becoming insignificant in this moment of being.

As you read this, turn your attention to body. What sensations do you notice? What does it feel like in this moment to "be body"?

A Minute for Me: Nothing To Add

There is nothing to add to that last sentence.

What does it feel like right now to be body?

Did you just read the last sentence or did you experience it?

What Is It?

My son Jon brought home a masterpiece from preschool when he was four. I had no idea what it was, but he was very proud of it. Made from the cardboard remains of paper towel rolls and empty tissue boxes, the sculpture looked like an odd monument to recycling, held together by what had to be a whole roll of masking tape. It was a boat, he proclaimed. "See the propellers, Mommy?"

When we retuned home, Jon decided the project wasn't done yet. I gave him more cardboard building material and another roll of masking tape, and he continued his work. "What are you building now?" I asked.

I gathered from his disgusted look that this question was a mistake. He rolled his eyes, clicked his tongue, and replied in an exasperated tone, "*Mom!*"

Watching him work, I realized that he wasn't striving to make anything in particular; he was just playing with form. He conveniently named the form as it morphed from one thing to the next. First it was a boat, then a pirate ship, then a skyscraper, and finally just a plaything that didn't need a name.

How often do I ruin the artful play of life when I prematurely ask myself the question, "What is it?" in relation to something I'm trying to figure out. The question takes the attention away from the process of creation and into the realm of labels and categories.

Like most people, when life dishes out a puzzle and I'm confused, I want to make sense of the situation, to put it into some sort of framework I can understand. Life, though, has a different agenda, letting the puzzle come together according to its own timetable.

We're all playing with life the way Jon was playing with his cardboard art, one piece at a time. The difference, though, is that Jon is quite content not knowing what's being created. What would life be like if you and I lived with that much trust?

A Minute for Me: Not Knowing

What do you think you should know, but don't? You've tried to figure out the answer, asked others how to solve the issue, took courses, and searched the web for how to put it all together. All to no avail. No rhyme or reason comes out of the pieces you've assembled from life.

Today, take a minute and see what it feels like to accept that the answer is not necessary for you to be happy now.

Can you force a flower to bloom before it's time? A flower blooms when the conditions are ripe, and not a moment before. Can you still enjoy the flower whether it has bloomed or not? What if we're like that? What if the answer we so desperately want comes when it comes, and not a moment before? How would you be in this moment without an answer to the question "what is it"?

Giving Advice, Living Advice

It's always easier to go with the flow if the flow is moving in a direction you like. It's also easier to dish out the advice to go with the flow if it's someone else's river, as I discovered recently.

It came to me when my husband was looking for a particular truck. We finally found just the right one and put a deposit on it. When I called the dealer back after a few days, he had some bad news for us. The dealership had sold the truck to someone else when our salesperson was off for a few days. My husband was not happy. I, on the other hand, was all tranquility. Maybe this was all for the best, I told him. Maybe we'd find a better truck for less money somewhere else. It had happened, I stated in a serene and knowing way, for a reason.

A few days later, I got a call from my book editor. The printer was behind schedule and the delivery date for the book had been pushed back. I was not a happy camper. What about the pre-orders? We have a distribution schedule to meet! I'll be away on vacation when the books are supposed to come! Couldn't the printer have foreseen this delay?

After I hung up the phone, I had to laugh. Remembering the advice I had so freely given my husband about his truck, I realized that advice is harder to live than to give.

What if the advice we so freely give to others is meant for ourselves? I want my children to be more patient, yet I hurry them to put on their shoes when it's time to go grocery shopping. I'm snippy and short when I ask my husband to stop speaking harshly to the children.

The thing I'm asking of others is the thing I need for myself.

A Minute for Me

Here's an experiment to play with today for your minute exercise. Every time you catch yourself giving advice to others, note it in your mind. Pay attention to what advice you are giving— either in your mind or out loud. How, in this very moment, can you live the advice you're giving to another?

If you can't find a use for your own advice in that moment, keep it top of mind. I promise you at some point today the advice you are giving others can be applied to a situation that arises today for you.

The Invisible Neutral

Semi-private yoga is a nice way to more fully explore the practice. With only two students, you're able to have a dialog as we moved through the postures, which is impossible in a large class. After we did some deep hip openers on the floor, we stood up and walked around the room, noticing what had changed in our bodies. What we noticed applied not only to yoga practice, but to life as well.

One student came into class with significant hip pain she described as "knives in my hip joints." Walking around the studio in inner reflection, she noticed that the pain had disappeared after she practiced the postures. The other student came to class feeling fine, yet noticed after the stretches that her hip flexor muscles were tight.

This is a perfect illustration of what happens in everyday life: Our attention is drawn to whatever causes us pleasure or pain. That which causes us neither comfort nor discomfort does not pull our attention. Neutrality makes it invisible.

This creates a bit of a dilemma. When the pleasure we're experiencing is over, we feel loss. When the pain subsides, we feel euphoric—until discomfort reappears.

As you read this, what are you conscious of? Do you notice pain in your back from sitting at the computer too long? Or perhaps you notice that your body feels healthy and energetic.

Notice aspects of this moment that are filtered because they seem neutral. Can you hear the beating of your heart, the clock ticking on the wall, the hum of the computer? Can your feel your feet, ears, nose, or other body parts that you don't usually notice? What does neutrality feel like?

A Minute for Me

Our preferences extend to everything we come in contact with, including people. Some people we like, others we don't, and some aren't even on our radar screen. Today's minute takes your attention to this preference that happens in the blink of an eye.

It's easy to notice when you feel that click of like-ability or the repulsion of dislike. What's harder to discern is neutrality. People whom we neither like nor dislike can seem invisible to us—people like the tollbooth operator, the bagger at the supermarket, or the stranger on the other end of the phone.

Notice today when a person threatens to become invisible because of your neutrality. Bring your full attention to them, turning them from invisible to the center of attention.

What happens inside you when you do this? How does it change your perception of this human being?

High Drama in Rooted Trees

With the shifting of seasons in New England, I feel the force of change pulling me. This transition between the high sun of summer and the dimming light of fall signals for me a new beginning, much more so than the beginning of a new calendar year.

With the sun lower in the sky and the leaves still on the trees, there is a sense of closing in. My body and mind react; I crave light and I feel a continual sense of urgency, leaving me with the impression that I should be making a decision, doing something, making things happen before the winter descends. It's as if I'm feeling the same anxiety our ancestors must have felt when the change in weather signaled the impending winter, and the need for survival drove a final, all-out effort to fill the storage bins. Do people in warmer climates have a similar reaction this time of year?

I'm uneasy in my body. I'm short-tempered, my mind is filled with things to do, and my attention is distracted. At the same time, I'm tired and just want to rest.

This is a season of in-betweens. Conflicting times. I see it played out in my body and in nature. In New England, this drama is enacted in high style, with the maple leaves gradually donning their costumes of bright orange and red, eventually bursting into a final flame of glory before being too quickly extinguished.

Even though it's high drama, I doubt the trees see it as conflict. It just is. It's simply the way of things. When inner conflict arises and our internal state seems as tumultuous as a tree blown by a hurricane, can the stability of a tree serve as a reminder to stay rooted?

There is a yoga pose called the Tree, a standing balancing posture. Just like trees in nature, people in Tree pose sometimes sway, fall out of the pose, or remain as steady as a rock. What if the "right" way of being in Tree, and in life, is just being with the pose as it is—swaying, falling, or stable?

My inner conflict during this season just *is*. There's no need to get alarmed by it, to fix it, or to change it. My guess is that my anxiety will fall away just like the leaves on the trees, following a natural course that I need not fight against.

A Minute for Me: Notice Nature

Take a short stroll in nature for your "minute" today. As you walk, scan your surroundings. Turn your head to see the full view of what's around you, staying open to nature's lessons.

What does the small sapling growing out of the cement walk tell you? What do mushrooms sprouting from a dead tree have to do with life? What quality does the nest-building bird display? How does a gentle babbling brook carve stone?

What does nature quietly whisper to you about living life?

Bill's Secret

I admire Bill, the financial planner. He's got it all together. When speaking at a local town meeting about divisive issues, his comments are well thought out, reasoned and logical. His approach to money management and home improvement projects are the same—methodical and consistent. He does his homework, and it shows. I bet he was an "A" student and a high achiever in school. Maybe even valedictorian.

Which is why I was excited that he was next to me at our hometown land conservation event. I wanted to pick his brain about his thought process. I was his opposite by nature—more creative than logical, more emotional than rational, more intuitive than reasoned. I had to work at developing skills that he seemed to exhibit so naturally.

As the biting October wind whipped through layers of clothing, I huddled next to the bonfire and chatted with Bill. Only in Hardwick would you find an event in the middle of a cow pasture, in the dark, on an incredibly cold and gusty night to celebrate land conservation.

It was in this unlikely environment reminiscent of a high school hidden beer party that Bill gave me his secret for keeping organized: a tiny, digital recorder he keeps with him at all times. With gusto he whipped the recorder out of his pant pocket and showed it to me by the light of the bonfire. He loved that toy, and told me eagerly how he separated his projects into different folders on the recorder. This audio folder is for home projects. This one is for work. This one is for miscellaneous items.

I bought a digital recorder at one point thinking it would help me get organized. It's buried in my closet somewhere.

My lists are everywhere. Food shopping lists are crammed into my pocketbook and in the kitchen drawer. Work lists are hanging on my office wall and in notebooks. Morning thoughts are scribbled on scraps of paper and laid on my dresser. Family chores and daily to-dos are inked on the white board on the kitchen wall.

I had lots to learn from Bill.

More than just mimicking a system, though, I wanted to know the answer to the most pressing question of all: Did Bill's strong organizational skills give him freedom and peace of mind within the whirlwind of tasks that make up a day?

He gave a small smile and answered by way of a story. One day, as the story is told, Bill wanted a break from work. He took a stroll through the Quabbin Reservoir—a gorgeous, pristine place in central Massachusetts that houses a grand lake for Boston's drinking water. Making his way down the path to the waterfront, he sat and watched the setting sun. He deliberately didn't think about work, and took in the scenery. Peace at last. That is until his reverie was broken by his own voice echoing through the air: replace the living room window, call Jack about the new account, change the oil in the car. . . .

His keys had accidentally pressed the "on" button for his recorder, which was now spurting out the litany of things he had to get done!

Many of us have minds that work like Bill's recorder, constantly reviewing and reciting the to-do list from sunrise to sunset. We wake up in the morning thinking about the things we are responsible for getting done. We go to bed at night ruminating about what else we need to do. We work on one project and think about the other project that waits for us.

Whether you are great organizer or a fly-by-the-seat-of- your-pants person, the bottom line is this: Do you have space, freedom and peace in this moment?

That list of yours will never go away. Cross one item off the top, add three to the bottom. It can suffocate and crush you if you believe the thought that it all needs to get done and that you're the one to do it.

In this moment right now, as you read these words, is your attention here? Or is the mind distracted by what else you "should" be doing or wondering what comes next?

Here's a suggestion: laugh at the list. That list is nothing, whether it is in the form of a very organized recorder, crumpled in your back pocket, or simply held in your mind.

That all-important list is nothing. You, on the other hand, are everything.

A Minute for Me: Count to Five

Hold your hand in front of your face, fingers open, with the palm facing you. Count to five, bending a finger with each count. Just for five seconds—the time it takes to move each finger—do nothing else. For five seconds, be quiet. Rest. Be alone. Be aware.

Breaking Habits

Habits are hard to break. I'm trying to break the habit of starting my workday with emails. When I jump right into email, it leads to a day-long link to the computer. The laptop and I become conjoined twins. This is day two of my attempt to start my work with writing with old-fashioned pen and paper instead of using technology. I cheated. While getting the kids off to school, I snuck into the office and peeked at my inbox. Okay, I confess I did more than peek. I also responded to a few emails, and that led to checking my blog, which led to me uploading a new video. Easing out of technology is like dieting—it's tough to eat less.

Just like cultivating a healthy eating habit, I'm back on track now, putting pen to paper— even though I feel pulled in the direction of gorging my email appetite.

Habits, I read somewhere, take daily practice over many weeks to become long-lasting. If the healthy eating habit is any indication, I'm a slow learner. I've worked many years to eat less since my maturing metabolism tells me I need less to maintain a certain weight. It's a habit I'm still working on.

I think it takes more than time to cultivate a new habit. It also takes tunnel vision. This same myopic view of the world came in handy when we took a family vacation to Alaska. The four of us enjoyed hiking but the terrain was very different than what we were used to in the Northeast. Here in New England, you have trees, making you feel secure as you ascend. You get glimpses of the vistas framed by maple or oaks. In Alaska, we hiked in alpine tundra. The views are breathtaking and vast. You can see for miles and miles all around for 360 degrees. This means you can also see below—leading to a dizzying sense of height. If the drop-off was steep, it was easy to become afraid. I noticed butterflies lifting my stomach into my throat on more than one occasion.

When my son Jonathan got nervous, my husband Joe had some good advice: look down at your feet walking on the path. This tunnel vision helped settle nerves. A myopic view blocked out distractions, focusing on one step at a time. Before we knew it, we were at the top of the mountain, feeling safe and secure, exhilarated by the accomplishment.

Joe's advice applies equally to developing new habits—keep your eyes focused on each step, and block out everything else.

This morning I looked around at the vistas and became momentarily distracted by emails from my newly developing habit of daily writing. When that view threatened to disorient me, I put my head down, and focused on this pen writing on paper.

Nothing else matters—not whether the writing is good or bad. It doesn't matter what, if anything the writing will be used for, or whether anyone will read it, or if there is other work that needs to be done. This writing is the path I am walking, leading to some unknown vista.

A Minute for Me: Distracting Vistas

What daily vistas are distracting you from a goal you have set for yourself? We all have things we want to experience or accomplish in this precious life. The sad part is many of us never get to it, instead becoming ensnared in daily stuff. Most of that stuff is not even meaningful to us. It's just a distraction. Today, practice the art of tunnel vision. Block out the dirty dishes and dance to loud music. Block out the idea that the car's oil needs to be changed right now and instead focus on a walk in the park. Commit to tunnel vision, at least for 60 seconds. That measly minute of tunnel vision builds a powerful concentration muscle.

Bad Moods Are Contagious

I caught my daughter's bad mood this morning. She's been away at camp every day this week, from early morning to dinner time, and woke up today tired and cranky. It wasn't long before I was cranky as well.

Ever notice that you can be in a fine mood one minute and a nasty mood the next, depending on someone else's behavior? It's almost as if moods are contagious, passed around like germs.

Can we build up an immunity to fight off someone's unhealthy temperament, like fighting off a cold? According to yoga philosophy, the answer is yes. When we become rooted in inner peace, knowing the truth of our existence, then our moods aren't at the whim of another's mood or any external circumstances. There are, I'm told, yogis among us who dwell in constant bliss.

I'm not one of them. But I have noticed that there are times when my children's behavior doesn't infect me, and I'm able to maintain equanimity (even if the behavior calls for decisive action). The observation that one can remain peaceful when someone else is disturbed is worth examining.

When you notice that you're remaining calm in the face of another's tantrum, magnify it in your mind. Really take notice of it. What is your inner state? How does the mind let go of that person's accusations, rather than engaging and reacting to them? What is the feeling in your body? Imprint that state of being in your whole body and mind.

We spend a lot of time and angst examining the pain in our life, focusing on what we need to change. And we usually beat ourselves up in the process, wondering why we can't be better than we are. What would happen if we magnified our moments of peace and contentment instead?

A Minute for Me: Three-Part Breath

Breathing patterns affect moods. To keep from getting infected with another's bad mood, focus on your own breathing.

Notice your breathing pattern now. Where is it going in your body? Is it smooth and long or short and shallow? Ragged or smooth? Is it tight or loose?

For sixty seconds, let's practice a new breathing pattern, which in yoga is called three-part breathing.

Sit in a comfortable position. Relax your shoulders away from your ears. Notice the thighs releasing into the chair, muscle draping over bone.

As you inhale through your nose, bring the breath first to the bottom of your belly. Then bring this same breath into your middle chest. Then complete the inhale by bringing it high into your upper chest, all the way under your collarbones.

Exhale through your nose in the same way—first releasing the breath from your belly, then your middle chest, and finally your upper chest.

Follow this rhythm with your own breathing cycle, taking slow, deep, even, and complete breathes. Expand and open your lungs to their fullest capacity. Deflate and completely release the breath with each exhale. See the wave you are creating with your breath.

How does breathing in this way affect your mood? How could you use it to build your immunity against bad mood germs?

Passive Will

When both my children started school full-time, it was the first time in nine years that I owned the hours between 8 A.M. and 3:15 P.M. I missed Jon and Emily, but I was very excited to dig into long-neglected projects. I had new, aggressive work goals, personal goals that had been ignored way too long (like losing a few pounds and going for more walks), and house goals that had been at a standstill (like getting the mudroom done).

So when the kids started school, I willfully charged forward. Progress, however, was *much* slower than I expected.

I get things done in my mind way faster than in real life. Will alone does not create the outcome.

We can play with the concept of will by looking at a yoga pose called Eagle. Like many balancing postures, it can be difficult. Most people tend to focus all their attention on the balancing leg, which causes tension. The practitioner tends to hold the breath, the torso wobbles, and the posture is full of effort. The result? Frustration and a feeling of inadequacy. Then comes the judgment: "I'm just not good at balancing postures."

The Eagle pose is a paradox of passive will.

Balance in the Eagle posture is not found by handing off the responsibility to one small part of the body. Rather, balance is found in the posture by engaging will while at the same time surrendering the whole body.

If you push the crossed leg firmly against the standing leg (using your full strength of will) and sink down deeper with the standing leg (surrendering the torso instead of holding on for dear life) you'll achieve an effortless balance.

Just as in life.

Using surrender and will at the same time is an absolutely fascinating idea with practical benefits. Think about it. How many times have you had to lay down the law with your children (strong will) but realize that you have to accept the fact that they are individuals with minds of their own (surrender)?

So you do what you can (will) and let go of the results (surrender). This is passive will.

What about at work? How many times have you pushed, cajoled, motivated, argued, and fought for a position that you believed in (using your will) only to realize you don't have the ability to influence the final result (surrender)?

The term "passive will" sounds like a contradiction. It seems impossible to achieve. Experience it in a yoga pose—or in life— and you'll know it's possible. You can use your strength of will to set goals, set a clear vision for your life, and move toward that vision every day. Then, in each moment, you can surrender to the actual experience as it unfolds.

A Minute for Me: To Will or Not To Will

The idea of passive will can be conceptualized as a definition, but the real power is realized through experience. The best way to experience it is to know the polar opposites that make up the whole.

For example, notice today when you are willful. During what conversations, situations and relations do you exert will? What is the energy of your will? Is it powerful and demanding or hopeful and clear? Is it direct and pointed or indirect and soft? Is it compassionate or crushing? How do you know you are exerting your will? When are you exerting will while trying to hide your will from another?

The opposite of will is surrender. Accepting the will of this moment means we stop fighting with reality. Notice today when you are okay with things just as they are, when there is no need to exert you will or make an effort to change the truth of this moment.

Is passivity easier or more difficult for you? During what conversations, situations and relations do you surrender? What is the energy of surrender? Does surrender feel like hopelessness or acceptance? Does surrender feel like relaxation or defeat? Does surrender come from a lack of caring or unconditional love? How do you know you are surrendering? When are you "trying" to surrender when really you want to exert will?

Get up close and personal with the opposite that is passive will, and see if you can notice when they both exist together in your experience.

Even while reading this, are you willing yourself to take these words to heart or is it a passive infusion? Or perhaps both?

A Minute for Me

A Perpetual Vacation

I just returned from a two-week vacation in Alaska. One of the best things about going away is coming home. For a split second you see your familiar house anew. There is a freshness about it. The wall color surprises. The squeak of the garage door opening sounds loud. The well water from the faucet tastes different than the bottled water drank while on the road. In chorus, everything sings "welcome home."

In the homecoming, the heart sighs, content.

Right after the contented sigh comes the rushing onslaught of tasks. I noticed the floor is filthy. Accumulated dust covers the shelves. Laundry from the trip is piled high. The fridge is empty so I have to go food shopping. Emails and phone calls need to be returned. Vacation is over, time to jump back into the fray.

I wonder, though, can the vacation mind set be lived in everyday life? Can one approach the daily habits and routines with a sense of adventure and exploration? Rather than being swept away in the expected norm of 21st century busyness, with all its technology traps, can I be more deliberate with how I choose to spend my day? Can a Monday feel as spacious and free as a summer day feels to a child?

Living a perpetual vacation calls for questioning routines. My normal routine at work is to boot up the computer, check emails, and jump into action. Most days, it seems as though the laptop is an extension of my body. I am attached to it for more hours than I care to admit. I limit the time my kids spend on the computer, yet I spend most of my workday on it—writing, planning, contacting clients, e-mailing. There is hardly a work-related duty that does not call for the computer.

When it comes to creating a vacation lifestyle, one of the first habits I have to question is the constant contact with technology. As I write these words, I hear another ding-dong bell coming from the laptop in the other room, challenging my decision to write this essay with pen and paper instead of tapping it out with the keyboard. That sound taunts, trying to lure me back into its grip. "Time to check emails," it whispers. "Come see what someone has sent you."

Taking a vacation is a choice. The physical separation makes it easier to make a mental separation from the constant tug of tasks. Yet I can make a choice right now and enjoy the wind and blue sky as pen flows over loose-leaf paper. I can make a choice to take a fanciful walk during the day just because I want to—rather than to "get exercise." I can choose to reply to emails and phone calls in a relaxed manner. I can choose to take my time cleaning the house. Or be okay living with a mess.

Vacation is a state of mind. This day was created for your enjoyment, not to ensnare you in the task trap. What vacation vistas can you see today?

A Minute for Me: Vacation for the Mind

What habits do you notice today? What actions are repeated day in and day out? As you notice the daily rituals, allow your mind to take a vacation from the routine by broadening your awareness.

Brush your teeth in the downstairs bathroom instead of the upstairs bathroom. If you take the same route to work everyday, allow your mind to notice a new tree, a different sky, or an uncommon radio show. As you enter your office, look around for something to be grateful for in the space.

Give your mind a vacation from the routine by switching it up.

A Minute for Me

Struggle for a Minute

This chapter of *A Minute for Me* is a struggle. I've started three times, dissatisfied as each fizzles to an incomplete end. I have a list of things to do, and I'm finding myself getting frustrated with my writing.

What do you do when a project stalls? Do you push through to make it happen? Do you give up? Do you do something else instead? Do you ask for help?

It's beneficial to look at our tendencies when we come up against an obstacle. It's not just the difficulty itself that deserves our attention. Our reaction to that obstacle is just as important to notice. Denial, repression, or forcing a solution just masks the underlying truth of our experience. The act of noticing the obstacle without buying into it takes its power away.

It's even better if you can harness the power of that obstacle. By writing about my struggle with *A Minute for Me*, I'm transforming the obstacle into part of the solution.

Instead of fighting with the problem you're facing now, can you use it constructively? Can a difficult boss teach you to stand up for yourself? Can a thankless job be an impetus to find rewarding work? Can a sore back be a reminder to take a break from the computer?

We all want things to be easy and pain-free. When I sat down to create *A Minute for Me*, I wanted the words to flow effortlessly. They didn't. Instead, each word was extracted slowly and painfully, like a tooth extraction before modern dentistry. Yes, we want life to be easy, but sometimes it isn't.

Sooner or later, though, the tide turns and what was difficult becomes easy. Before you know it, you've overcome the obstacle, just as I've overcome my struggle with this chapter and come to the very last word.

A Minute for Me: Dissolving Obstacles

There's a constructive and a destructive way to approach an obstacle. Obsessing, dramatizing, emotionalizing or having a tantrum over an obstacle strengthens its position. Objectively admitting its presence and continuing forward nonetheless decreases its power. Before consistent and conscious action, obstacles wither.

Today, when obstacles arise (as you know they will) neither ignore nor indulge them. Take sixty seconds to simply acknowledge their presence, and move ahead.

A Steady Commitment

This week I asked an entrepreneur what most surprised her about starting her own business a few years ago. I can relate to her answer: the need for steadfastness. The need for staying the course.

I remember one of my favorite jobs back when I was in college. I was a pharmacy technician, a job that was fast-paced and finite. At the end of my shift, when the store closed, my task of helping the pharmacists fill prescriptions was done for the day. The counter was clear, all the work was complete, and the next day could begin with a clean slate.

That's not the case with most things in life. The tasks of an entrepreneur, a business executive, or a parent are never really done. Like laundry, these tasks go on and on. You never experience the feeling of being "finished." Rather than the get-it-done, cross-it-off-my-list mind set, many aspects of life call for steadfastness—a continual, disciplined plodding that brings results over time.

Steadfastness delivers no immediate gratification. It's not glamorous. But the long haul has its own rewards, which are not always readily apparent in our bits-per-second world.

The ancient sage Patanjali defines *asana* (the Sanskrit word usually associated with the physical postures in hatha yoga) as a steady, comfortable pose. Steadiness and comfort enable us to keep an intended focus for a long time. They give us endurance. We experience a different inner quality when we're steadfast as opposed to when we just want to get something done. Steadfastness calls for continual commitment to a purpose you deem important. It's the opposite of the "I just want to get it over with" mind set.

What fills your mind—tasks that create steadfastness and growing commitment, or tasks that you just want to get done?

A Minute for Me: Focus on Intention

Today's minute is one of my favorites. When you wake up in the morning, take a minute for yourself, just setting the stage for how the day will play out. Forget the list that pops up in your mind of this task or that. Instead, focus on your intention for the day. Notice how the body transitions from sleeping to waking.

How do you want to be in this day with yourself and with the people around you? What would you like to feel today? In what ways are you grateful for this new day? What words of thanks could you give to the sun for rising this morning?

Rather than being task-driven first thing in the morning, what does it feel like to be intention-driven and gratitude-driven?

The Image in the Outline

There were big happenings in the small town of Hardwick this past weekend. The Hardwick Fair, the longest running consecutive country fair in the United States, was in full swing. It's not your usual variety of fair, the kind with cotton candy and Ferris wheels. It's an old-time version with kettle corn and sheep shows.

This year, as they do every year, local artisans showed their wares. One particular painting by an artist named Frank Bly caught my eye. It depicted an American Indian woman cradling a child in her arms. What was different about it were the raised swirls all over the canvas, outlining the image of the woman and child. Even after staring at it for quite a while, I could not figure out how Bly had done it. The outline of drizzled acrylic looked so natural and smooth it had to have been applied free-form, without too much thought to the image itself. But the Indian woman and her child fit so well into the outlines created by the acrylic drizzle that I was convinced the picture must have been preconceived.

I asked the artist about his process for creating such a beautiful image. His answer: the border came first. He took the acrylic paint and randomly drizzled it over the canvas. After it dried, he took a close look at it and saw the picture that was already present in the lines. Staying as true to the outline as possible, Bly then used his painting ability to bring out the image.

I love this process as a metaphor for life. How often do we really look at the overall outline of our life, and see where our skill can be used to naturally draw out what is already there? Many of us struggle to create the life we want, pounding and hammering like a blacksmith forcing hard metal to his will. If our day were a pattern, what picture would emerge? If we are unhappy with the picture of our life, can we paint a completely different image within the same outlines?

Woven through the seemingly random events of everyday life is a grand design, waiting to be discovered.

A Minute for Me: Borders

What are the borders within which life unfolds for you? For me, the borders of family life and personal interests drive the picture I'm creating on this canvas. What about you? What borders do you work within? Are you satisfied and fulfilled with the container or border that you create from? That border might be a responsibility, a physical location, or a mind set, a belief, or a faith. Can you see the border clearly enough to work around it and with it, rather than fighting it?

Bring Peace to Your Pace

Jonathan was in no hurry to go to kindergarten. In fact, the more I tried to push my then six-year-old son along, the slower he went. The orders I gave—*eat your breakfast, go get dressed, brush your teeth*—fell on deaf ears. He moved like cold molasses. I heated up, moving faster to keep him from missing the bus.

Then I had an idea. Setting the kitchen timer, I suggested, "Jon, let's see how fast you can get dressed." Squealing in delight, he raced up the stairs, threw off his PJ's, and got dressed for school. Then he was back down again, skidding to a halt in his socked feet and panting, "What's my time, Mom?"

At what point in life do we change our minds about time, turning it from a fun race into a frantic pace? Can time be a friend, helping us accomplish what is most dear to us, or are we destined to forever fight against its passage as we try to squeeze more and more into 24 hours?

Time is simply the movement of the sun across the sky, broken into segments we call hours. Break that movement down into smaller segments and we call it minutes. Slice it even smaller and we have seconds. Time is an arbitrary system to which we have become slaves.

Time is like money: we never seem to have enough. And this continual shortage leads to a sense of lack in our hurried lives. How can we make more time?

The answer is simple: we can't. You and I and the rest of the world all get the same twenty-four hours each day. And since time was devised by the human mind, the only way out is to use that same human mind to bring peace to your pace.

The concept of time is very useful for one thing: helping us make choices. The most important choice in life is where to place your attention. Where you place your attention dictates where your energy flows, which in turn determines the actions you take. A diffuse and distracted attention results in diffuse and distracted actions, which in turn create a diffuse and distracted outcome. By deliberately choosing where to place your attention at any point in time, you can take appropriate action, shifting from continual reaction to a life of conscious creation.

Then time mastery becomes self-mastery.

A Minute for Me: The Biggest Time-Sucker

For most of us in the working world, e-mail is a voracious time eater whose appetite is never satisfied. The ding of the Inbox pulls at your attention like a black hole's gravitational pulls at the universe. Today, choose to give your attention to e-mail in timed mini-bites. Set a timer for ten minutes. Your mission, should you choose to accept it, is to move as many emails out of your Inbox as possible in that allotted time. You MUST stop at ten minutes, no matter where you're at. You can file, delete, or respond to the e-mail. But you only have ten minutes.

Did I mention that you only have ten minutes?

This exercise is like when you are getting ready to go on vacation. The mind becomes very focused and gets done a huge amount of work in a short period of time. There is no dilly-dallying. Well, you are employing the same technique here.

After the exercise, take a minute to reflect. What did you notice about your attention? Did the mind wander? What was the outcome? How did time help you? Was there a negative side to timing? In what way could you harness time for your greatest good?

A Minute for Me

A Stake in the Ground

I'm busy organizing my disaster of an office. Sorting through old files, sticking my to-dos in a neat new file organizer, and recycling reams of paper, I can finally see the top of my desk again. I guess I would do just about any task this morning to avoid what I should be doing: writing this essay. Sometimes this writing task seems daunting. What should I write about? Any other task looks more appealing—including the dreaded chore of cleaning out my filing cabinet.

Talk about desperation.

Sometimes when we're not sure what to do, doing something is better than doing nothing.

At a meeting last week, a woman told me she was torn over a decision. Should she be looking for a job in another state, where her family lived and needed her support, or should she stay and look for a job in town?

Whether you're writing an article or looking for a job, it helps to put a stake in the ground, a stake that proclaims, *Here is where I'll start, in this very moment.* My avoidance tactics can give me lots of energy, since buzzing along cleaning up my desk feels so productive—see how nice it looks now? And perhaps avoidance is a necessary step in the process since, after all, it *is* helping me to write this essay. But sooner or later I have to get started, even if I'm not sure where I'm going to start.

When we put a stake in the ground, committing pen to paper or putting a resume in the mail, the action puts the universe on alert. It says, *I'm moving forward, I'm ready to take action.* The universe, of course, answers in unanticipated ways. In my experience, the stake in the ground never leads to what we expect.

There are two yogic precepts that guide this process. The first is self-knowledge—the ability to question your assumptions, explore the mind games that limit you, and ultimately know the truth of Self. The second precept is surrender—the ability to accept that we don't have all the answers and that the universe will take us to places we didn't foresee.

Put your stake firmly in the ground, knowing full well it will be ripped up. Then you'll pick it up and plant it once again.

A Minute for Me: Walking

Walking is something most of us do everyday without even thinking about it. Each step is like putting a proverbial stake in the ground. As your heel, then arch, then ball, then toes touch the earth, a direction arises. A path is set out and the next foot naturally follows.

Take a minute and walk with conscious awareness. Feel the feet making contact with the earth. Notice as a direction is set and the path is followed. Walk with a purpose. What happens when you walk this way?

Danger in the Middle of the Road

Recently I taught two yoga classes for my friend when she wasn't feeling well. Substitute teaching has its disadvantages. For one, I'm not familiar with the students' physical limitations and needs. I spent time on the phone with my friend, asking her about the levels of her classes and having her fill me in on anything else I should know.

Later that night, I introduced myself to the first group of students, who my friend had told me were at a beginner level. I chatted with them and let them know what type of class I would be teaching. When I mentioned that this would be a beginners' class, there was opposition. No, they said, they were more experienced than beginners. They put themselves at the intermediate level.

With the next group, I told them I'd be teaching an advanced class, as my friend had recommended. No, they said, they weren't yet advanced students. They put themselves at the intermediate level.

There is perceived safety in the middle of the road. The word "beginner" connotes inexperience, knowing less than others. Being "advanced" means having lots of experience, knowing more than others. One position requires a willingness to ask questions; the other a willingness to answer questions. Either position can feel vulnerable.

Yet the middle of the road holds its own danger—the danger that you will languish in a comfortable place that offers little opportunity for exploration.

Buddha instructed that the middle path was the way to happiness, avoiding the perils of extremes. Yet always following the middle path is in itself an extreme. There are times when you're called upon to be the expert. There are moments that call for your beginner's mind. Whether you're comfortable as an expert or as a beginner is irrelevant. The question is whether you'll choose comfort and stay in the safe middle, or choose courage and explore the edges.

A Minute for Me: The Un-comfort Zone

Are you more comfortable playing the expert or the beginner? What role do you usually play?

Today we are going to switch it up a bit. In a role that you usually play the expert, play the beginner. For example, maybe as the boss, a presenter, or a parent, you are used to telling people what needs to be done. What if you played the beginner and asked questions instead of giving answers?

Or, if you have a role where you play the beginner (or follower), practice taking the lead and give direction. Offer a vision, suggest a path forward. Be an authority.

How do these roles affect your inner state? How do they affect your relations and interactions with others? What would it be like to flow through the day being the beginner sometimes and the expert at other times?

A Minute for Me

Do You See What I See?

Tresca glanced at the revised website. In the time it took me to read the first paragraph, she had already pointed out three spelling mistakes on the page.

Walking down a country road, Joe stopped short. While I was enjoying the stroll, his sharp eyes had spotted a wild mushroom well off the road, hidden in the woods. He had to take me within inches of the fungi for me to see it.

What hones one person's attention, enabling them to see something that is invisible to others?

As it turns out, Tresca is a talented and trained editor. When I asked her how she had spotted the mistakes so quickly, she explained that misspelled words just pop out at her, even before she's had a chance to consciously read the material. Similarly, Joe is a wild mushroom connoisseur who has hunted for edible fungi for years during his many jaunts in the woods.

Through discipline, study and practice, they have trained their minds to be alert for certain subtleties that most of us have to work hard to see—if we spot them at all.

What have you trained your mind to see in life? Could there be something right in front of you, right now, that is life-altering, but invisible to you?

There are teachers who have taught that we are sleepwalking, that there is a holistic truth to this existence that we are missing, a truth that lies invisible and hidden beneath our own identity: our true nature is bliss.

I'm cranky today and rather ticked that this truth is hidden. It's a cruel joke that I can be pure bliss and still be bothered by PMS.

Siddha yoga master Swami Muktananda said, "God dwells within you as you." Others have spoken similar words. The truth of who we are is as close as our breath—it is the essence of who we are—yet we completely overlook it as we busily move through our daily existence.

As Joe identifies a mushroom hidden under a rotting tree, and Tresca points out how two letters have been transposed in a word my brain automatically fixed while reading, I can't help but wonder how to train the mind to see the invisible that Jesus, Buddha, Muktananda and others have realized.

How can one study what is beyond lessons? How can one practice that which is beyond systems? How can one understand a concept that obliterates concepts?

Maybe we start where it all begins: in the mind. For 60 seconds, turn your attention inside and watch your thoughts. How many of those thoughts create an identity called you? Who would you be without those thoughts? What new thing would be revealed right in front of your eyes?

A Minute for Me: The Gift of Sight

It's easy to give others credit for what they see naturally; to appreciate what they have honed, practiced and perfected in their life.

Sometimes we can be blind to our own gifts.

What do you see today that others may be blind to? What gift of sight have you honed to see your specific perspective in this world?

As you move through the day, notice the patterns you create, the connections you observe, and the pictures you make in your mind. Your perspective is as unique as your fingerprint. Your exact perspective only comes about once in eternity. It's a limited edition. In fact, it's the only edition. There's not another to be found in infinity. Can you feel the preciousness of your perspective?

A Minute for Me

Candy at the Country Store

Coffee was calling for me at the country store. I listened. As I poured a cup of java, Jonathan looked around for a snack.

Now, if you are familiar with country stores in any town, you know that they are jam-packed with candy. Not lined up in neat little rows on white wire racks like they are at the chain convenience stores, but tucked in odd aisles and crammed onto wooden shelves.

This did not make Jon's decision any easier. When you're in kindergarten, choosing between a whoopee pie and a giant pixie stick can be the biggest decision of the day.

I took my time preparing my coffee, occasionally asking Jon if he knew what he wanted. "Not yet, Mom," he replied each time.

I stirred the coffee. Chatted with other customers. Sipped my coffee. Still Jon poked. I was growing impatient. "Do you know what you want, Jon?" I asked for the hundredth time.

He gazed at me with those sweet brown eyes, a look of distress on his little face. In a dramatic moment that should have won him an Oscar, he wailed, "Mom, my life is one big 'I don't know'!"

I can relate. The question "What do you want?" can be tricky. Can you answer it?

From seemingly small decisions (like what entrée to order) to the big decisions (like what you're creating with your life) not knowing the answer can be scary. And they can be as fraught with emotion and drama as Jon's struggle to choose between gummy bears and a PEZ® dispenser.

When you set out in one direction, life often comes up with another.

That's the truth of it when you try to answer the question "What do you want?" Sometimes you decide. Sometimes life answers it for you.

When faced with the "I don't know" mentality, why struggle? Why force yourself to find an answer, or to hurry the process along, or to try to fit everything in? Try riding the "I don't know" wave and see where it takes you. Maybe somewhere as sweet as Jon's gummy bears.

A Minute for Me: Wanting

For today's sixty-second exercise, let's play with the concept of wanting.

Think about something you want. What does that thought process look like? Is the path to get to your desired goal crystal clear or does thinking about how to get there just confuse you? Is there a paradox of choices, making naming what you want difficult? Are there too many action steps needed to get what you want, making you exhausted just even thinking about it?

When you want, what happens to you?

Does the act of wanting create a feeling of something missing, or of something coming into being?

A Minute for Me

Holiday Bliss?

Ah, the glory of the holiday season. This is the time when families gather around warm fires and sip hot cocoa—not the instant kind you nuke with water but the old-fashioned kind you make with milk warmed on the stove. Stockings are hung with care and trees are trimmed while carols are being sung. Children's cheeks are rosy from sledding, and good cheer fills the heart and home.

Until, of course, Mom has a meltdown over the never-ending shopping list filled with people she has no idea what to get and Dad throws the Christmas lights on the floor, unable to find the defective bulb that's holding the whole strand hostage. Like a bad thriller movie featuring the sweet guy who turns into a demented killer, Christmas cheer transforms into holiday hell.

It's all fun and games until someone gets poked in the eye.

Here's my personal interpretation of the hectic life: Its job is to build constructive attention. What are you paying attention to? To hear the quiet whisper of truth in a rock-band-volume life takes great discipline and nerves of steel.

For me, that discipline is not a display of brute force in which I push myself to do certain tasks. Instead, it takes the form of questioning, observing, and listening. Some questions I've been playing with as I ponder my own direction include:

What is my mission in life?
What drives and motivates me to do what I do?
From where do I take my direction?
What is the source of my decision-making?
Given that, what are my priorities for the New Year?

What step-by-step process do I follow to get that done?
Who can help me with those steps?

Each year I go through a business and life planning process. Sometimes I plan with a group, sometimes alone. Some years the plan is detailed and long, other times short and sweet. Sometimes I pay someone to help me create a plan of action, other times I do it myself.

One thing I know for sure: The form of the plan doesn't matter in the least. What counts is the clarity, focus, and peace the planning process brings to my mind. The planning process, not the plan itself, is the gem. Through the process, I spend time questioning, considering, and listening instead of doing, implementing, and taking action.

Once you have given yourself permission to sit with the possibilities and dream about the potentials, your mind finds freedom instead of getting trapped listening to a broken record that keeps squawking about what needs to be done. The planning process develops constructive attention.

Here's a real-life example.

When I reflected on the questions above, it was clear that more discipline was needed for my writing. So I set aside Monday mornings. Today was the first day I was scheduled to start, and the kids have a snow day. Instead of quiet writing time, I have a sick son hacking away and a daughter begging me to go to the store and get more Christmas lights for the tree she wants to decorate (yes, my husband actually did toss down the string of lights in frustration—and if I am to be completely truthful, I have had a meltdown or two lately).

Despite all this, I'm writing. It is not at all like I'd planned (it never is), but I am choosing to focus my attention on this word right now. I hear my husband and daughter arguing, my son is coming over looking for attention . . . and I notice that I have finished this sentence.

Now I'm off to give my attention to my son, get lights for the tree, and otherwise dive into the holiday truth as it unfolds in my house.

May your daily truth be one of peace and love, even if the occasional meltdown blows apart the fairy-tale myth of the perfect family gathering.

A Minute for Me: Pay Attention

Where your attention goes, energy flows. That's why we're constantly exhausted during the holidays—our attention is focused on everyone else, our energy drains out and we become depleted. We have just allowed our self to become invisible to our self.

The solution is simple: pay attention to you.

Notice your socked feet against the floor as you make breakfast, feel your breathing as you rush to the mall, notice the sensation between the top and bottom jaw at the business meeting, observe the softness of your child's hand in yours. Even as you read these words, notice your shoulders. Can they drop further away from your ears? Paying attention to you means that even when you are giving to others, you are rooted in yourself.

All You Can Eat

Most of us want to get our money's worth when we're at an all-you-can-eat buffet. I've noticed I pile more food onto my plate in these situations than I ever would order from a menu. There is, after all, no doggie bag for later.

Many of us look at time the same way we look at a buffet. We cram in more and more, wanting to get it all done in this lifetime. We say yes to a new project because it excites us. We say yes to the community committee because we feel obligated. We say yes to leading the after-school program because we want to spend quality time with our children. We say yes to extra tasks at work because we think it's our responsibility. Our plate of life is piled high.

Let me state the obvious: it's impossible to give adequate attention to everything if there are simply too many things on your plate.

If you continually overeat at a buffet, you eventually become overweight. If you try to spread your attention among too many tasks, you eventually become stressed-out and ineffective.

Where is your attention now? Perhaps you are feeling the pull of tiredness, the sense that there is another book you'd rather be reading, or that you should be doing something else altogether (like folding the laundry, making dinner, or preparing for work). This split attention creates the feeling that you don't have enough time.

What are you choosing to put on your plate?

Take a long hard look at your commitments. What would you choose to leave off the plate? What do you want to keep? Once you've made your choices, give 100 percent of your attention to whatever's left on your plate, and savor every bite.

A Minute for Me:
Enough for One Lifetime

Write your response to this question: when are my tasks done *enough*? Instead of finishing, when is the project *done enough* in this moment?

We tend to define done as finished, complete, all over. Is anything ever really done? Or does life just change it up into something else?

Can you live peacefully in the unknown abyss of never-ending? Or live with curiosity about the always-new beginning?

If life is always beginning, and nothing ever ends, what would be the impact on your all-important list of things to do?

The Writing Life

I'm sitting here this morning in my favorite writing chair—a mission-style recliner with wide wooden arms that have plenty of space for my coffee. Later I'll add the cordless phone to the other armrest for my business calls. It's rather dangerous. I could sit here for too long. My strategy is to consume lots of fluids, forcing me to get up and take care of business when my bladder insists upon it.

I love the writing life.

I hear a cacophony of birds outside my open window and the frogs in the pond croaking their satisfaction. It's summer, so instead of a roaring fire keeping me company I have tame votive candles in the fireplace.

The geese honk loudly when they arrive in the spring and again when the leave in the fall. They fly so close to the rooftop that you can hear the noise echo down the fireplace flue. Sometimes I leave the comfort of my writing chair to watch them. I love when they are so near I can hear the powerful flap of their big wings move through the air.

In the poem *Wild Geese*, Mary Oliver writes, "Whoever you are, no matter how lonely, the world offers itself to your imagination, calls to you like the wild geese, harsh and exciting over and over announcing your place in the family of things."

What would you write today as the world offers itself to your imagination?

Writing gives me the time to actually see this moment—to take note of what's happening in the unfolding story words create. It's like the writing creates a new reality, one that was invisible before when I was busy doing instead of noticing.

Appreciation of what's right in front of you arises when you write.

Writing focuses your attention. Sometimes that focus brings clarity as the story reveals a little more of itself. Sometimes that focus just brings up more questions—where is this story going? But the writing always gives a surprise. "Look," the words say, "I've just spun a new world that didn't exist thirty minutes ago."

Writing is the big bang theory in action. Not here one moment, here the next. Writers are Gods, creating worlds with words.

There's no better way to spend the day. Or the next sixty seconds.

A Minute for Me:
For the Next Sixty Seconds, Write.

What would you write now as the world offers itself to your imagination?

A Minute for Me

Mental Magic

This morning I woke up fuzzy and with a headache. I slept well last night, but I felt hung-over. No, it wasn't because I had overindulged at a wild party. It's been a long time since I've attended anything that could be classified as "wild". I'm fast asleep before anything remotely resembling wildness starts. The reason for this hangover was a little less spectacular. I'm cutting down on sugar.

Again.

Halloween spurred me into action. What sick, twisted mind came up with the idea that giving away a *gazillion* little chocolate bars to sugar-crazed kids (and parents) was a good way to celebrate? Of course I do my duty and get a bag just in case any kids ever come to our house in the boonies (they never do). That bag gets eaten before Halloween, so I get another. If there is candy in the house, it somehow mysteriously shows up in my hand, all unwrapped and ready to go. At which point I, of course, pop it into my mouth.

It's the Halloween curse. . . .

So again I find myself needing to interrupt the sugar cycle of craving, overeating, feeling lousy. Sugar likes to take advantage of me. Maybe I'll conquer the sugar sickness some day and leave for good. For today, though, I'll be happy with maintaining a healthy boundary.

I decided to make myself a cup of herbal tea called "Mental Magic" to rid myself of the sugar withdrawal brain fuzz. I steeped a whole pot. Later, a friend asked if the tea was working. I opened my eyes wide in surprise saying, "Oh, yeah, I forgot to pour it!"

A Minute for Me: Make Your Own Energy

The sugar habit is hard to break because the buzz is quite nice. Like coffee (or drugs for that matter) sugar gives a nice rush, followed by a crash that leaves you craving more. And eating more never satiates that craving. It's a vicious cycle.

Today for your Minute, consider generating your own inner energy and high, versus looking for it in a chocolate bar. Take a run, go for a brisk walk, or practice this simple yoga posture.

Stand with your legs hip distance apart, feet parallel. Lengthen up through the torso, feeling the full height of the body from the tips of your toes to the top of your head. Pretend to sit in a chair while handing a tray to someone standing in front of you.

Your arms go straight out in front, with your shoulder blades tucking down and back instead of straining forward. Bend your knees generously, keeping them parallel and over the ankle. Stick your bottom out to the wall behind you as if you were preparing to sit in an imaginary chair.

You should feel your thighs working (come out of it bothers your knees). Stay in the pose as long as you can, coming in and out until you feel the heat and energy arise. Remember to breath.

When you're done, notice. What's the energy like in your body?

Crash That Party

I crashed a party this weekend and got kicked out.

Well, it was really more of a business meeting than a party. Even so, the bouncer—in this case a high-powered female entrepreneur instead of a burly barman, showed me the door. The messenger was different, but the message was the same: you are not allowed here.

As the group of professionals gathered around the meeting table, a man spoke to the woman in charge, saying, "There are some people that don't belong here."

I was nabbed.

In front of the entire group, I was escorted out. Like a teenager being shunned by the cool in-crowd, I was embarrassed, hurt, and angry.

Would I put myself back into that same position again? You bet. In a New York minute. I wanted to learn from this group, and I was willing to break a few rules to do just that.

How about you? Would you put yourself in a place you didn't belong, with the threat of getting kicked out, just to learn? How far would you go to learn what you want to learn? To do what you are being called to do?

Computer genius Bill Joy—the programmer who wrote much of the software that allows you to access the Internet and the guy who cofounded Sun Microsystems—broke school rules about allotted computer time. So he could spend more time learning programming, Joy exploited a bug in the software, giving him unlimited access to the computer. This open learning vista gave him the practice needed to accomplish great things later in life that both you and I benefit from.

Bill Gates broke school rules about allotted computer time. So he could spend more time learning programming, Joy exploited a bug in the software, giving him unlimited access to the computer. This open learning vista gave him the practice needed to accomplish great things later in life that both you and I benefit from.

Bill Gates broke the rules to learn. As a teenager, he would tiptoe out of his house in the wee hours of the morning to walk to the University of Washington, where he would steal more time on the computer. Between the hours of three and six in the morning, young Gates practiced playing the computer the way Beethoven practiced playing the piano—for hours and hours over years and years.

If you want to learn more, if you have a calling you're following, rules, regulations, certifications, documentations or diplomas don't mean nearly as much as the actual doing. That's why Gates and Joy broke rules to do the computer stuff they love.

That's why I break rules to do the entrepreneurial stuff I love.

It's the doing that calls to you. And that call is much louder than the warning bells to follow the rules. .

Life is full of rules, and people will always be happy to share why this rule applies to you.

What rules are you willing to break to learn what needs to be learned? To do what is being called for you to do?

The whole world will scream at you, "Don't do that! You're breaking the rules!"

Do you listen?

What rules are you living by—yours or others?

Go ahead, crash a few parties. Get thrown out. Get rejected. Feel embarrassed. Do a little "this-is-so-unfair" dance. Let your inner child have a self-righteous tantrum.

Then turn your attention inward. What's next? Because it's not about participating in parties that others are throwing. It's about throwing your own party. And that party is called your life.

A Minute for Me: The Rejected Partygoer

Think about a time in the recent past that you've been shut out. What were the circumstances? What was your response? How did that rejection pave the path to where you are now? Where you might go in the future?

It's easy to fixate on rejection. The shun can feel personal. It can feel like a door closing in your face, leaving you feeling powerless and victimized.

What if that rejection was the opposite? What if it was, and continues to be, an invitation to delve deeper into yourself, to really commit to your heart's desire?

Inspirational Quotes

This morning I went to add a new saying to my "favorite quotes" folder and found that the file was gone. I've been adding to that document for over a decade, collecting all the sayings that touched my heart, gave me inspiration, or provided a new perspective. Now the inspirational document is gone—probably accidently erased when I was cleaning up the hard drive.

It's like a metaphor for life. Sometimes we lose inspiration.

I am not happy about the loss of the document. Maybe I'll search through my backups and see if it was somehow captured there, although that just feels like too much of a distraction right now.

But then inspiration struck . . . .

Why not ask my blog readers to share their favorite quotes? That way, I could start a whole new document, and we could share as a community our favorite quotes that inspires us. We would all benefit!

That's exactly what I did. Now I have a new file, populated not only from my own explorations and inspirations, but also from a like-minded community of friends.

You can see what people wrote, or add your favorite quote here.

Inspiration strikes at odd times, and sometimes when you're feeling low (like when data is lost). The loss forces you to think differently, to try a new approach, to consider a way around the obstacle. I had no idea I was going to write a blog post asking for help on quotes until inspiration struck with the loss of my inspirational document (that irony is not lost on me).

Following your inspiration when it arises ensures that more will come. Why would inspiration visit if it kept hitting a brick wall?

The quote I was getting ready to add to my lost document came from a good friend and business colleague. She had sent me a beautiful card when my beloved sister passed away. It included a Sufi quote which read:

> The heart weeps for what it has lost;
> The soul laughs for what it has gained.

It's the first quote I added to my new "favorite sayings" folder. It sums up the way of it—the soul knows something we don't.

A Minute for Me: Let Others Help

When you feel at a loss, you can listen to your inner inspiration, and you can ask for help from your community.

Take the next sixty seconds to journal using free-association, no-holding-back writing on an issue where you feel blocked. Use this sentence to prompt your writing if it helps:

I'm lost. I have no idea what to do about . . . .

When you're done, reach out. Call a friend. Talk to your partner. Write a blog post (if you want the whole world to help). Do something that signals you are open for ideas. Then watch, listen, and take in all the wisdom that comes your way.

Mom, Your Life is Boring

My son Jonathan was home sick this week, so he got to hang out with me. He saw first-hand what I do during the day – doing the laundry, writing, recycling, returning books to the library, talking on conference calls, and working on the computer, among other things. By day three, he was well enough to go back to school, and sick and tired of my daily routine.

When I asked him what he thought of my activities, he looked at me sideways with his eyes slightly rolled up, as if disgusted. "Mom" he said, "you lead a very boring life."

Such is the glory and adoration of motherhood.

He's right, of course. I've often thought that myself as I'm picking up his dirty socks. It must be very freeing to whip off those socks at the end of the school day and fling them to far corners of the room or under the couch.

Life as an adult means responsibility, and that can definitely be a big bore.

As I write this I'm sitting on my back deck. The laundry that's never done is hanging on the clothesline. It must be seventy degrees — very warm for the first week of April here in New England. It feels like we've moved right into summer and skipped over spring.

The neighbor's rooster is crowing. The songbirds are twittering, and the dryer is humming with the clothes I didn't feel like hanging on the line.

I suppose you could call this boring. But I'd much rather be doing this than sitting in a classroom like Jonathan, or working in a cubicle.

Whether you're going to school, have a high-powered executive job, doing Mom things, or simply writing, it can all look boring from the outside. And it can feel boring at times on the inside.

Boredom has some redeeming qualities that are easy to overlook in our desire to be entertained.

Boredom can come from doing the same thing over and over. That's called practice. Maybe Mozart got bored with composing. Or Amelia Earhart got bored of flying. Or Bill Gates got bored of computers.

It may look exciting from the outside, but boredom happens in every human life. It's part of the human experience.

In his book, *The Outliers*, Malcolm Gladwell wrote that getting to be the best at something has to do with the magical number 10,000.

Give any skill 10,000 hours of practice and you'll be an expert at it. In that period of time, I bet you would feel bored at some point and want to give it up for something more exciting. And maybe your son would tell you that your life is boring.

Sometimes boredom can be a wake-up call, inviting you to do something exciting, new, and adventurous to break out of a routine. But sometimes boredom is just the price you pay to get really, really good at something you value. Then a day comes when you surprise yourself by your level of expertise, not really sure how that brilliance came out of such drudgery.

I still don't see how picking up dirty socks can lead to an expertise (and I really don't care to be an expert at housekeeping, thank you very much). But I can see how showing up for the writing day in and day out, even when it's pure drudgery to do so, makes me a better writer. That's a skill worth working at in my book.

What are you practicing over and over again? What's the skill you're willing to be bored with as you work towards the 10,000 hour master level?

During the course of a life we're all spending that amount of time on something — whether it's 10,000 hours of complaining, living deliberately, building a business, or mothering.

Whether or not you find it boring at times is not at all important. It's just part of the journey. The real importance is that thing you're giving your 10,000 hours to cultivate. Is it a skill you feel is worth it?

A Minute for Me: Acknowledge Mastery

Many times mastery shows up quietly, without us even realizing we were cultivating the skill. What you're great at can be invisible to you and obvious to others. It's easy for us to dismiss an expertise that seems commonplace after 10,000 hours of practice.

Take walking, for example. When was the last time you gave yourself credit for being a master at taking a step? It's no small feat (pun intended).

And if you don't walk, are you a master at sitting up?

Today, acknowledge mastery in your life, whether your mind classifies that mastery as "important" or "not important". Practice saying to yourself, "I can do that."

The Blank Page

I bought another journal today that I didn't need. My daughter says I have a fetish for journals – and she's probably right. I have thin and fat, large and small, colorful and plain journals stuck in all sorts of places – including by my bed, in my car, the office, kitchen and here now as I sit on our town common at the local farmer's market.

I like the blank pages bound with a beautiful cover. It holds potential. It's unencumbered with rules, responsibility and "shoulds". It's filled instead with "possibles."

We all need a pathless place to explore—like a coloring book without lines, an empty book, a blank canvas, a walk through the uncharted woods.

Maybe the infamous mid-life crisis comes when we deprive ourselves of a space to just create. When we keep reaching outward for satisfaction – a fancy new car, a thrilling young relationship – we miss the creative inner spark that is the sustaining, interesting and intriguing juice of life.

Do you ignore the capacity to be led from inner motivation versus outer expectations?

It's not easy to meet the blank page; it's scary and at times cumbersome. But it's infinitely more satisfying. And that type of satisfaction lasts longer than the fleeing high of the shiny new thing used as a distraction.

If you looked at your day today, would you find space for a blank page? Is there room in your mind for creative expression without boundaries? What would you do with that space if found?

A Minute for Me: Summer in Seconds

Take the next sixty seconds to bring summertime energy into your heart and mind.

Sitting quietly, perhaps where you can have the sun on your face, close your eyes and let your mind wander back to carefree summertime days. Allow your open mind to gather images of summer.

Without controlling, notice if one summertime memory is brighter, stronger, or louder than the rest. Settle on this memory and focus your attention on it. Notice how old you were, the energy in your body, the thoughts in your mind, the smell in the air, the colors of the sky. Bask in the summer fun.

When it feels right, thank the memory and open your eyes. What part of the memory can serve you as you create in this day?

Creating Community

I had no idea if teaching yoga to seniors would suit me. I thought I would be overwhelmed managing the physical limitations, or perhaps bored with a gentler practice. As it worked out, though, I absolutely love the two senior yoga classes I teach each week at the senior center. They are the highlight of my day.

The most pleasant surprise has been the bonding of community. There's a genuine concern for each other's wellbeing. There have been many medical emergencies, such as hip or knee replacements. Just last week, we had a 92-year-old student leave via stretcher after a dizzy spell. But through illness, death, and celebrations, we're here for each other.

No matter what you're able to do physically, you are welcomed into this class.

You may find a ride to class when your car breaks down. Or receive a card in the mail when you've been sick. Or get a phone call if you haven't been to class.

This strong sense of connection and community has got me thinking—how can you and I foster this support in all aspects of our life?

There are lessons to be learned and gifts to be received when we look upon every interaction throughout the day as a way of building community. In community, we support one another. We challenge one another. We find laughter and lightheartedness with each other.

Just today I was riding down the road to pick up some fresh corn on the cob from the farm down the street (there's nothing better than corn just picked that very morning). On the way there, something flew off the car in front of me. I stopped the car and picked up a hat that the driver must have left on the roof. I recognized the car as my neighbor's, and I knew I could get it back to him. Then I noticed he had turned around, and was coming back in the opposite direction to claim his missing chapeau. I slowed down, reached my hand out the window and waved his hat.

With a big grin, he grabbed the hat in transit like the ring at an old-fashioned merry-go-round and yelled, "I love my little town!"

That's the essence of community—when you know your neighbors and help each other out.

Bottom line: in yoga and in life, it's more fun to practice together than alone.

A Minute for Me: Know Thy Neighbor

Do you know the person who lives next to you? How about two doors down? Three? How far down the road do you have to go before you get to a house where you don't know the person who lives there?

Do you feel a sense of belonging in your community?

How could you be more connected? In the next sixty seconds, come up with a list of possible actions to be more engaged in your community. At the end of that exercise, pick one item that resonates for you, and go out and do it.

A Minute for Me

The Definition of Yoga

If there was a person on earth who had never before encountered the wind, what words would you use to describe it? Could any terms fully explain what it feels like to stand atop a mountain while mighty gusts try to blow you off balance? Would words do justice to galloping through a field on your horse while the wind whipped at your torso? Or sticking your hand out the window of a traveling car to feel the incredible force pushing at your arm?

All definitions and explanations are sadly lacking. They are mere shadows of the actual sensations.

You could try defining the wind by explaining what it does – such as how the wind moves the hair off the nape of your neck, how it feels like light feathers brushing across your skin, or how it makes you happy on a hot summer day or scared during a violent thunder storm. The wind's effect gives us a better sense of how wind works in the world, and is certainly much more revealing than the definition you'll find in the dictionary: "current of air."

Defining yoga is a lot like defining the wind: It's much more effective to communicate the effects than to nail down a concrete definition. But even beyond describing the mental, physical, and spiritual effects of yoga, the best way to really know "yoga" intimately is to experience it for yourself.

Wikipedia defines Yoga as "a healing system of theory and practice. It is a combination of breathing exercises, physical postures, and meditation that has been practiced for more than 5,000 years."

Like defining the wind, that definition of yoga leaves me uninspired and tired.

For some reason, we're always trying to define yoga. Maybe we think a definition will somehow validate or codify the experience of yoga. But capturing the wind, or yoga, within the confines of a definition does the experience an injustice. Definitions, by the very nature of the defining act, exclude. Yoga and meditation, on the other hand – like the wind, the sun, the moon — are completely inclusive.

If you want to experience wind, go to where the wind usually shows up, like a mountaintop or the ocean. If you want to experience yoga, then practice asana, explore breathing techniques, or chant a mantra.

Yoga is to be experienced, not defined.

I've noticed anytime I have had a profound yogic experience, my ability to wrap words around it makes the experience slip away. The mere act of trying to put what is beyond words into the confines of words diminishes the memory of the experience. But if I just remember the experience, without needing to capture a definition, the memory comes alive.

That's why the definition of yoga is such a trap. Each person brings their own concept to defining an individual experience of wholeness (and yes, even that word "wholeness" is a trap.) Thousands of years ago, someone pulled out that Sanskrit word "yoga" (which means "to yoke" or "to unite") and said "this is what we'll call this practice."

Since we haven't figured out yet how to communicate telepathically, we're stuck with words. Let the words and the definitions of others be an open invitation to your own inquiry. What is yoga (or your spiritual practice) for you?

A Minute for Me: Drop Definitions

When we see a tree, we mentally label it with a four letter word spelled T-R-E-E. Those letters create the word that creates the mental concept that defines the thing.

Try to look at a tree and not see it as a tree.

That same process holds true for anything and everything. As soon as we define, we confine.

For the next sixty seconds, take in "all" the world. Let your lens open wide. At some point a label may arise, like labeling a noise as a barking dog or labeling the current of air as the wind. When a label does arise, mentally counter it by repeating the word "more".

After acknowledging "more", go back to taking in "all" the world around you.

A tree is more than a tree. You are more than your body.

Why Go Down a Dead End?

Looking up at the steep hill, I saw the "Dead End" sign. Well, I wondered, why should I work that hard to walk up a hill only to turn around and walk back down again?

Normally, I would not have wasted the effort. Today was different.

Given that I had just dropped my daughter off for a three-hour gymnastics practice and I had to wait for her to be finished before taking the hour's drive home, there was time to kill. So I turned in the direction of the hill.

I wasn't quite sure why I made the effort now. I could have continued my walk on the flat terrain, but I didn't. Perhaps I took the more difficult path because my mind was twisting thoughts in the same way you would twist a Rubik's Cube® to get the right answer. As a business owner, there's always some puzzle to figure out, some problem to solve, or some new initiative to evaluate. I was mulling over one business problem on this day and could use the distraction of physical effort.

The hike up the steep dead-end street was just the ticket.

I made my way to the top and turned around. The view was spectacular. I could see well across the city. In this dead-end little side street, it was very peaceful. The noise from the busy city below did not carry up. And although it was indeed a dead end, it was much longer to the end than I anticipated.

I felt invigorated. Dead end or not, it was well worth the effort.

That got me to thinking: Do I overlook the virtues of taking a dead-end path in life because I judge it to be "useless" or a "waste of time"?

When you get right down to it, is any road, or any action, ever really a dead end? Isn't there always something there of value, something that made it worth the effort, some learning that would otherwise not be gained had the dead end not been taken?

For that matter, why do we call it a "dead" end? There's no death here. Only us noticing what there is to notice along the way. Then we turn around to take another road. Isn't that the way it works whether the road is a dead end or not?

When we make a decision and decide on a path, there's absolutely no way to be sure if a dead end lies ahead. Even if every sign screams that the road is a dead end, we may find when we arrive that there is an exciting path that is little traveled but holds great promise.

As the last couple of lines of the poem *The Road Not Taken* point out:

> Two roads diverged in a wood, and I —
> I took the one less traveled by,
> And that has made all the difference.

Would Robert Frost still have taken the path less traveled if it was labeled a dead-end?

Trying to track out each and every path on the road of life — including the roads we meander down as business owners — is an impossible task. We think because we map it out, the path is clear. But we know from experience that as soon as we head down the supposedly open road, we can hit unexpected construction, an accident, or a nice view that we want to visit with for a while before we move on.

The supposedly open road can be a dead end. The dead end can be an opening.

At the heart of it, every road is just a journey.

A Minute for Me

Take the next sixty seconds and look back on the trajectory of your life. What are all the little twists and turns of fate that have brought you here to this exact spot?

Are the times in your life when you labeled something as a dead end, but looking back you can see how it opened new doors in the future?

Do you feel like you are stuck in a dead end now? Could even this dead end be a new beginning?

.

800 Pounds of Bad Mood

Rocky was in a snit, probably because the spring bugs had sprung. They buzzed across his ears and eyes without mercy. A teeny bug is not intimated by an 800-pound horse in a bad mood, but I am.

I was trying to do him a favor by taking him out of the paddock and into the field where the fresh green grass was sprouting, but the bugs followed us. As I held the lead rope loosely, he stepped on it, effectively pinning his own head down to the ground. He immediately started complaining by pounding his other hoof into the earth. Still trying to help, I reached down to lift his leg to pull the rope free. He protested and ended up with the rope caught on his horseshoe.

Sometimes trying to help a crabby horse (or a crabby person) is a thankless job.

Rocky was getting even more bad-tempered. With his head still pinned down and the rope still stuck on his shoe, I decided the best course of action was to just let go. In short order the snag came undone, but Rocky was threatening to bolt — not a good idea with the rope still dangling. It could trip him up and he could end up seriously hurt.

I tried a few times to reach for the rope and that just made him act like a three-year-old with a tantrum — you can't catch me! So I changed tactics. I just stood and talked in a soothing tone, "What's the matter, are the bugs bugging you?"

He calmed right down and I reached for the rope, upon which time I brought him directly back to the relative bug-free zone of his stall.

His predicament made me think of my own life.

I have the sneaking suspicion that I've pinned myself down plenty of times. It is, of course, hard to see for yourself when you're the one causing yourself grief. It's like trying to see a blind spot, just like Rocky couldn't see that his own hoof had pinned the rope and thus his head. The tendency is to pound the ground in frustration, grow impatient, and turn away from the hands that would have helped had we but allowed it.

Sometimes all it takes is the willingness for another to be quiet with us during trying times, to speak gently and soothingly to us, to abstain from giving advice about how we should do this or that to get out of the knot we've made, for us to unknowingly untie the knot ourselves.

A Minute for Me: Pinned by Deadlines

Deadlines are like Rocky's lead rope—they make it easy to pin yourself down.

They can be a motivator to get things done or an exhausting burden of responsibility.

How many deadlines do you have in your life? Are they energizing or draining?

How do you unwittingly pin yourself down with deadlines? Do you regularly overcommit or create unrealistic timelines?

Today, look at deadlines like Rocky's lead rope—are they trapping you in a place you don't want to be, or a means to a fresh pasture?

It's Raining Responsibility

We celebrated my daughter's sweet sixteen birthday with a weekend in New York City for just the two of us. One plan of many squeezed into a short 48 hours, was to grab a cup of coffee and have breakfast near (instead of at) Tiffany's. We got rained out, though. The rain poured down in buckets, pounding at our umbrellas as we waded down the street to the Metropolitan Museum of Art. Around us, those that didn't have umbrellas ran for cover. Looking at someone splashing by us, my daughter said, "Mom, do you know you get wetter running through the rain than just walking?"

I actually didn't know that, and asked her to tell me why. Apparently, the TV show Myth Busters did an experiment on running in the rain (yes, I know, where do they come up with these ideas?). The myth they were trying to confirm or bust was whether running kept you drier. It did not. Over a hundred-yard course, the data from eight trials showed that the running person got wetter than the person walking.

As I thought about that little factoid, I couldn't help but relate it to life.

There are some people that always seem in a rush, hurrying through life to get onto the next thing. I know what that's like—I do it myself at times. Like trying to stay dry by running in the rain, it's been my experience that running through life gets you soaked with stress.

It's the rare person that walks with grace and ease through life, even when it's hailing down responsibilities that make most hurry. When I see people barraged but still calm, or when I'm able to stay in that relaxed state despite it all, I study it.

It's a unique skill that calls for attention. Those people stand out. Good leaders have that ability, as do good parents.

You would think that when Chesley B. "Sully" Sullenberger crash-landed into the Hudson River in New York that his voice and demeanor would be rushed. Yet recordings of the radio traffic showed that the pilot was extraordinarily calm during the entire event.

You would think that the Mom in the grocery store dealing with a terrible-two tantrum would be harried and rushed. Instead, without a word, she calmly picks up the child and leaves the store, coming back after a time-out restored peace.

Circumstances happen every day where a rushed response could immediately arise.

In fact, as I try to concentrate on writing this morning, other requests are bombarding me. My son wants to have a friend over to visit. My husband is coming in and out the house getting ready for work. My consulting client has an immediate need and wants my input right now. My daughter is waiting for me to take her to get her haircut for back to school.

Can you relate?

When I do come back to the writing, can I do so in an unhurried way? When you feel rained on by life, can you walk instead of run?

A Minute for Me: Notice the Downpour

I wonder if the harried and hurried pace we sometimes find ourselves in is because the mind is jumping ahead of where we are now. The mind can time travel, but the body is firmly rooted in the here and now.

In today's minute, take note of the mind when life is in a downpour. Close your eyes and notice:

1. What's the physical response of so much stimulation? Where does it show up in your body—as a tight belly, or short breaths?

2. Where is your mind, focused on the task your body is doing right now, or on all the other things waiting for your action?

3. How would your experience change if you mentally walked instead of ran through this moment?

A Minute for Me

Comparatively Speaking

Everything about the giraffe's body is built for one thing: reaching towering heights. As the world's tallest land animal, they have an unrivaled reach. With legs that are taller than many humans—about 6 feet—to a neck that weighs over 600 pounds, the whole structure enables the giraffe to eat tasty treats unavailable to others constrained closer to earth.

Yet you don't see other animals lamenting the fact that they can't reach what's easy for the giraffe to reach. The zebra or lion don't appear to be jealous. You don't see them being melancholy over the fact that they are height-challenged in comparison.

It seems a purely human trait to compare ourselves to others, only to find ourselves lacking in one way or another.

I do consulting work at Kripalu Center for Yoga and Health, the largest and most established retreat center for yoga, health, and holistic living in North America. On any given day, I can look around the cafeteria during lunch to see lots of fit, young bodies. I notice my mind comparing my middle-aged body that gave birth to two children to those younger bodies.

Those thoughts are, of course, useless. But they are there none-the-less.

Wanting to cultivate a peaceful approach to my maturing body and do less comparing, I shared my experience with a friend of mine. I wanted some advice from this wise woman I admired. We chatted as we walked the grounds of Kripalu after lunch, confirming that yes, indeed, no matter how well you eat, no matter how much yoga you practice, the body ages and changes.

It's like the shirt I saw on an older person in the Kripalu cafeteria. It read, "I eat well. I exercise. And still I'm gonna die."

Well, that's it in a nutshell, right?

As my friend and I walked, we started laughing. Unfortunately for me, I did not take a bathroom break before our walk. So as our giggles ramped up, so did my need for a stronger bladder muscle. Since those muscles have never been the same since giving birth, I improvised. I did what every woman instinctively knows to do—I crossed my legs and squeezed.

There I was, right in the middle of the picturesque road leading to a meditative retreat center, hunched over my crossed legs hysterically laughing for everybody driving by to see.

Which only made us laugh all the harder. Then my friend let out an unexpected burp.

All we needed was a good old fart to finish off the image of two aging bodies out of control.

All ended well. I made it to the bathroom without incident, and my friends excess gas had been worked out. And the laughing fit continues to nourish me anytime a thought arises about the maturing process. If I can still laugh hysterically because of bathroom humor, all is not lost.

Even as I write this essay, I am laughing hysterically. Laughing really is the best medicine.

Yes, the giraffe can reach great heights. But what happens when he wants to get a drink of water? His height hampers. He becomes vulnerable to attack as that long neck that can reach the heavens cannot reach the earth, causing him to spread his legs wide or even kneel in order to drink. In fact, the giraffe's jugular vein contains a series of one-way valves that prevent the back-flow of blood when the head is down to drink water to prevent a black-out.

No great gift like the height of a giraffe comes without a corresponding downside. The great gift of maturity is perspective. The downside is a weak bladder.

I can handle that.

A Minute for Me: What's the Blessing?

Today, notice when you are comparing yourself to someone else in an unfavorable way. What is it you're comparing—a body, a brain, an athletic skill?

Take whatever you are comparing and write it down on a piece of paper. Set a timer or your watch for sixty seconds and write down as many blessing as you can for the thing your comparing.

For example, if you are comparing bodies, list out all the blessings your body provides—the ability to feel, taste, touch, smell, laugh, hug, jump, play, etc.

Anytime we focus on what's lacking in a comparison, we miss the blessing. Choose today to focus on the blessing.

Dream Big

Inspiration struck at the grocery store. I was heading for the checkout counter when my eye was caught by a photo on a greeting card: a darling baby with her bright, sparkling eyes peeping over the top of a bucket, above the words, "Give us dreams a size too big so that we can grow into them."

I bought that cute card.

Dreams are never meant to be toned down to what is reasonable, comfortable, and in a size that fits you now. Dreams need to be bulky, unwieldy, a bit too big to hold, with plenty of room for a growth spurt or two.

Dreams are meant to be bold.

For some reason, growing up seems to translate into growing out of big dreams. Youth seems well suited for energizing pie-in-the-sky thinking. Growing up usually means replacing big thinking with "being realistic"—a known killer of creativity.

Like Goldilocks looking for just the right fit, reaching out for your dreams means trying new things on for size so you are constantly stretching your heart and head. Dreams don't need to be limited by anything as mundane as geographic or financial constraints. They just need something simple to be nurtured—they need a "yes" from you instead of a "no".

Saying "yes" to a dream means answering the call. Dreams are always calling, whispering of a new way, a creative possibility, a grand adventure. Dreams require many "yeses" and "I do's" along the way. Just like in any committed relationship, you don't say "I do" once and walk away. Everyday actions either solidify that "yes" or break it apart.

Your dreams are worthy of that daily "yes," aren't they?

A Minute for Me: I Have a Dream

In order to say "yes" to the dream, there first has to be an acknowledgement that a dream exists. And sometimes we are so worn down from the daily grind that dreams disappear.

Today you are just going to give space for dreams to bubble—without censoring, squashing, or ignoring what arises. You are going to give voice to the dream.

Find a private place, maybe in the bathroom in front of a mirror. Smile, look at your reflection, and say this sentence out loud, "I have a dream that someday…"

Then take sixty seconds to voice as many big, impossible dreams as you possibly can.

Conclusion

The year, and this book, is coming to an end. I'm writing this last chapter just before the holidays. I'm sitting on my recliner in front of the fireplace, with roaring flames holding the cold New England air at bay. It's toasty. Right outside the door, though, the temperature is a chilly fifteen degrees.

Sitting inside the house feels very different than being just ten feet away outside the house. A person right next to you can have a radically different experience than you. Each perspective, each place in space, gives a fresh outlook. That outlook is as unique as a snowflake.

From where I sit I can see the decorated tree where each ornament tells a story. There are fragile, antique glass teardrops from my mother-in-law's collection that we inherited after Joe lost his father to cancer (his Mom passed away several years before, also from cancer). There are cute, fun ornaments that appealed to the kids when they were younger—like Barbie and Batman. Now we have football players and flipping gymnasts. Even the candy canes draped over the branches tell a story. Every year after Thanksgiving my family takes a trip to a local candy store. There they roll out the candy canes by hand, snipping the long taffy roll into smaller segments with a pair of big scissors, and then curve the top over to make the hook while the candy is still warm.

The tree tells our family story. Although our perspectives are different, the four of us that live under this roof have a common, shared story. It's amazing to think that all of us—the whole human race—share a common story. A unique perspective comes from every human across all corners of the globe and forms our collective story.

Under the tree are the wrapped gifts. Come Christmas morning the wrapping paper will be littered across the living room floor and the mystery will be solved. The kids will finally know what was hidden. Until then, though, we're in the dark. I say "we" because even though I wrapped most of the presents, I can't remember what they are! So we see the gifts, are excited about the possibility of what lies hidden, and look forward with eager anticipation to find out what's beneath the layers.

We each have our own perspective. We each come together in this shared story called living a human life on planet earth. And we can live that story with a deep sense of excitement and eagerness as the mystery reveals itself one small peek at a time (or perhaps even a big rip open).

May this moment of your life be a treasured gift, just waiting for you to open it to see what's inside.

About the Author
Head above the clouds, feet on the ground.

People with big ideas face a constant challenge: how to transform that vision into a new and better reality. Whether it's change in your personal life or success in your business, vision needs action (and rest) to manifest.

Megan McDonough follows three principles to transform your big idea for life into reality:

+ Get clear with yourself – and others – to get results
+ Take the natural next step – finding balance organically
+ Fast-track past the status quo by cultivating constant curiosity

Mastery of "how to get from Point A to Point B" is her trademark, whether it's leading Kripalu Center's entry into online learning, speed-launching a first-of-its-kind worldwide virtual conference, creating award-winning executive sales techniques, developing consumer wellness products, or teaching thousands of people to live with ease and clarity based on their own internal compass.

A Minute For Me rests on the lessons that this yoga-teaching mom has distilled from more than twenty years of sales and marketing leadership in the largest healthcare companies on the globe, entrepreneurial success as a health and wellness consultant, trainer and writer, and as a committed practitioner of mindful living.

A national media source for *Fast Company*, *Yoga Journal*, and *Woman's Day*, Megan is an explorer at heart, uniquely prepared by her own professional and personal adventures to help you navigate the tricky path between dreaming about what's at the summit and actually climbing Mt. Everest.